World-shaped Mission

World-shaped Mission

Exploring new frameworks for the Church of England in world mission

Janice Price and the World Mission and Anglican Communion Panel

CHURCH HOUSE PUBLISHING

Church House Publishing
Church House, Great Smith Street,
London, SW1P 3AZ

British Library Cataloguing in Publication Data

A catalogue record for this book is available
from the British Library

978 0 7151 4290 5

GS 1865

Printed and bound in Great Britain by
CPI Group, Croydon

Contents

Part 1 – Theology and Practice for Mission 1

Part 2 – Developing New Mission Practices 41

Appendices

In memory of Tom Heffer and Christopher Jones
who, in their own ways, contributed much to this project.

Foreword
by the Bishop of Bristol

I wholeheartedly welcome the publication of *World-shaped Mission*. It provides an important assessment of the journey the Church of England has travelled in negotiating our place in the Anglican Communion and the worldwide church in the last 50 or so years as well as providing pointers for the future.

It is the fruit of a three-year process that has been driven by the World Mission and Anglican Communion Panel together with the World Mission Policy Adviser, Janice Price. At the meetings of the Panel different perspectives have been brought to the discussion from the Anglican Communion and the global church, the ministry of both of our Archbishops, our ecumenical partners, the Mission Agencies, Diocesan Companion Links, the Development network and from the life of the parishes of the Church of England. *World-shaped Mission* represents a weaving together of these many and diverse perspectives.

The overall message of *World-shaped Mission* is that the Church of England needs to move towards a greater mutuality in world mission relationships through a process of giving and receiving that enriches all and enables the church here at home to participate in God's mission more purposefully. No one is under any illusion about how difficult this is and the deep differences that can exist between churches in different parts of the Anglican Communion. However, it is a journey that we are part of by virtue of our history and that we shall be part of into our future.

One of the greatest strengths of *World-shaped Mission* is that it provides a process through which parishes are enabled to build their understanding of and engagement with the church globally for the purpose of enabling our participation in God's mission here at home.

I am grateful to my colleagues on the World Mission and Anglican Communion Panel for their support and input into this process. Together, we are grateful for the wisdom, input, hard work and good humour of Janice Price without whose know-how and effort this publication would not have taken place. We are gratefully indebted to her.

I commend *World-shaped Mission* to the Church of England.

The Rt Revd Mike Hill
Chair, The Anglican Communion and World Mission Panel
Mission and Public Affairs Division of the Archbishops' Council

World Mission and Anglican Communion Panel

Chair

The Rt Revd Mike Hill, Bishop of Bristol

Church of England representatives on the Anglican Consultative Council

The Revd Rose Hudson-Wilkin
Elizabeth Paver

Partnership for World Mission Agency Members

Church Mission Society – The Rt Revd Tim Dakin (until February 2012)
United Society for the Propagation of the Gospel: Anglicans in World Mission – Janette O'Neill
The Mothers' Union – Reg Bailey
Church Pastoral Aid Society – Revd Canon John Dunnett
Mission to Seafarers – Revd Canon Huw Mosford
Associate Mission Agencies – David Friswell

Other Members appointed by the General Synod

Dr Jackie Butcher, World Development Advisers Network
Revd Canon Roger Matthews, Companion Dioceses
Revd John Kafwanka, Director for Mission, Anglican Communion
Revd Canon Cynthia Dowdle, Companion Dioceses

In attendance

Revd Canon Joanna Udal, The Archbishop of Canterbury's Secretary for Anglican Communion Affairs
Revd Dr Daphne Green, Chaplain to the Archbishop of York
Revd Dr Malcolm Brown, Director of the Mission and Public Affairs Division of the Archbishops' Council
Janice Price, World Mission Policy Adviser

Summary

Narrative – The Church of England's world mission relationships are expressed in many forms. The long history of the work of the Mission Agencies represents stories of sacrificial service to God and neighbour and a deep commitment to the gospel in England and in the wider world. This sacrificial service has contributed to the growth of the Anglican Communion and still bears fruit today. However, against the background of British colonial influence, of which the Anglican Mission Agencies were a part, though a not uncritical part, various unintended consequences of such missionary involvement emerged. These unintended consequences were an over-dependency on the ways and culture of the Western churches and the disruption brought to indigenous spirituality and culture as the result of foreign presence. With the demise of British colonial influence, there has been some awareness of the need to move beyond patterns of dependency and the Church of England continues to work through that process. The question is being increasingly asked: What would it mean to shape world mission relationships based on mutuality and equality? This is the essential question considered throughout this report. As English society continues to undergo rapid change, the Church of England ministers within cross-cultural contexts here in England. This has brought an urgency to the need to learn from partners in the global church.

Theology – The immediate post-colonial language for world mission relationships is partnership as an expression of God's mission in the world. While this has opened up many aspects of working together there is a need to find a language that will help all partners move towards greater mutuality. With Jesus Christ at the heart of God's mission, participation in the life and mission of Christ through the Holy Spirit, together with exercising gracious hospitality, are concepts that require further exploration in mission theology and practice. Hospitality carries the strong connotation of welcoming the other (Christ as both guest and host) and participation focuses on our common calling in God's mission in the world. The emergence of the prophetic strand of God's mission in the world is opening up new realities of the Church's calling.

Practice – The process of moving towards mutuality is already being actively considered in the Mission Agencies and the Companion Links at diocesan level but attitudes of donor/receiver and dependency are proving to be resilient. There is a need to intensify this process through attitudinal and structural change. Long-term **attitudinal change** involves recognition of the need for Anglican Christians to see themselves as 'cross-cultural Christians'[1] in their own context. **Structural change** involves an examination of our current world mission structures concerned with co-ordination (Partnership for World Mission). The arguments for having a co-ordinating function for world mission include:

(a) the necessity for co-ordination in a field of increasing diversity

(b) the importance of a sense of common Anglican identity

(c) the need for continuing relationships with the National Church Institutions

(d) the need to be seen to be working out principles of mutuality among Church of England Links and Agencies as well as with our partners in the global church.

---

1 There are already many resources to help in this process not least those produced by the Mission Agencies. A set of benchmarks could be developed through which cross-cultural awareness could be assessed. Many in our parishes encounter those from different countries and contexts. However, the key process is turning the experience of encounter into the transitions that transform discipleship.

Currently Partnership for World Mission provides a light structure focused on the development of strategic relationships. However, in the current financial climate funding the co-ordinating structure remains problematic.

The Church of England is not alone in seeking to move towards greater mutuality in world mission relationships. In the West the majority of British denominations are considering similar questions though with particular denominational expressions and approaches. Likewise many in the European and North American churches are making similar journeys. In the Majority World churches continue to be established and grow. They ask that their voice be heard in the Western churches.

Part 1 – Theology and Practice for Mission

Chapter 1

The Mission Imagination

Summary

This chapter locates the heart of mission in the person of Jesus Christ and the work of the Holy Spirit as the primary revelation of the mission of God the Holy Trinity. It goes on to outline how understandings of mission have changed over time and outlines some of the different understandings of mission today. It explores what factors are shaping how the church currently imagines mission. The conclusion is an encouragement to the Church of England to stretch its theological imagination to see new ways of engaging in world mission.

> 'Mission is jazz, the exploration of the new and the creative out of the strength of what is laid down by participants who know expertly how to play their instruments.'[2]

1.1   Prophetic mission, integral mission, holistic mission, frontier mission, reconciliation, liberation and justice, the Five Marks of Mission, to name only a few, are all helpful descriptions of mission and all attempt to gather what often seems like a varied and disparate set of activities. There are many different ways to think about God's mission in the world. God's mission is practical, earthed in the local and about real needs and lives. Throughout Christian history as the church has reflected upon God's mission and been creatively led by the Holy Spirit in imagining new ways of expressing God's mission it has come to understand mission differently according to local context. Whatever these different descriptions give us they, like jazz, explore the new. So mission today uncovers new questions about God's work in the world. However,

> 'this jazz is not just an experiment or whim, but emerges from a thoroughgoing knowledge of the tradition'.[3]

One definition of mission which acts as an umbrella for many others understands God's mission as the overflow of the love and life of the Trinity into the world.

1.2   Today, as the Church of England considers the different patterns and shapes of world mission over history so now is a time for stretching the mission imagination and seeing the emergence of new patterns and creative shapes. It is about being in tune with God's imagination as the Spirit moves in the world. This involves taking the past seriously and learning for the future. With the vast changes in world relationships the church worldwide faces a particular opportunity for new shapes of relationships to emerge. Such a moment is called a kairos moment. One way of expressing this is through the term 'Ephesian Moment',[4] which refers to the time when the Jewish and Gentile ways of expressing Christian faith became one and where there was a realization that each needed the other to be the Body of Christ. Today, Walls states,

---

2 *Presence and Prophecy*, Introduction, Churches Together in Britain and Ireland, Church House Publishing, 2002, p. ix.

3 *Presence and Prophecy*, p. ix.

4 This term is adopted by Andrew Walls, 'The Ephesian Moment', in *The Cross-Cultural Process in Christian History*, Orbis Books, 2002, pp. 72–81.

there are many more than these two understandings of how to live the Christian life. However, the principle holds in that all expressions of Trinitarian faith are 'equally necessary to realize the fullness of Christ'.[5]

1.3 **Jesus Christ – the heart of mission**

The church today explores God's mission in new contexts but what is the tradition from which we come? The heart of mission and the tradition which Anglicans inherit and inhabit is an understanding of mission based on the presence and proclamation of Jesus Christ in the world as the full and complete expression of God's mission and the continuing work of the Holy Spirit in the world. As stated earlier, God's mission is the overflow of love of the life of the Trinity into the world. The love of God has its complete expression or outpouring in the Incarnation.

> 'In the Incarnation, God's own mission and ministry become one, for God does not simply cause or intervene in human affairs, but becomes fully human interacting with the human condition at every level.'[6]

The foundation of all Christian mission is the mission of God fully expressed in Christ's coming to earth. Christ's coming was a threefold movement or action of the Trinity which also involved human partners and has done in every age. Christ's being on earth had three inter-related elements, as explained below, which are at the heart of how we understand mission today.

1.4   The first aspect of Jesus' mission is **presence.** Christ's presence on earth was the birthing of a new order. His was a presence that brought both transformation and disruption to the lives of many of those on the margins of society and to the lives of the powerful including those of the religious leaders of the day. Today, Jesus Christ's presence is also one of suffering or identification with the world in its brokenness as well as the means of salvation through the work of the Holy Spirit. It is through Jesus Christ that the world is connected with the reign or the Kingdom of God. The second element is **proclamation** where the presence of Christ proclaims the new order which is the Kingdom of God through word and deed. This is the rule or reign of God in the world with which Christian mission today is primarily concerned. The third element is **prophecy.** Christ's presence and proclamation points to a new way of living and being and as such is prophetic. It envisages new ways of being and living in the Kingdom of God in accordance with God's nature and supremacy. This is the reign of God which points to a future beyond the dichotomies, injustices, glimpses and tastes of the Kingdom in this world. The end of all things and the fulfilment of Christian mission will be the point when all things will be brought together in Christ (Ephesians 1.10). So God in Christ is both the author and fulfilment of all Christian mission and is the embodiment of God's mission here on earth. Today through his resurrection life and by the presence of the Spirit in this age, as the director of mission, the Kingdom of God will be ushered in which will see the fulfilment of God's loving purposes for all creation. Returning to the image of mission as jazz, this is the ultimate theme on which all the variations and improvisations of God's mission on earth is based.

---

5 Walls, 'The Ephesian Moment', pp. 72–81.
6 *Presence and Prophecy*, Introduction, p. 27.

Imagining mission and differing narratives

1.5   How does the Church of England imagine God's mission in the world? How does the church think of mission in our current age and context? For Anglicans who regularly worship in parish churches what comes to mind when they hear the word 'mission'? What possibilities does that word hold or what negative images does the word 'mission' evoke? Contexts differ and change. The dominant image of world mission for some in the Church of England would be mission in places other than England. However, that image is being seen increasingly as a thing of the past. Through Fresh Expressions and other initiatives, the Church of England's mission imagination has been stretched to see England as a place where God's mission is happening as well as in other parts of the world. How we imagine mission, however, emerges from our experience of our discipleship. We respond to God's generosity to us in Christ and how that is expressed in the service of God's mission in the world.

1.6   Jesus expressed the way he imagined God's reign largely through the parables. The parable of the Wedding Banquet (Matthew 22), for example, gives a glimpse of the invitation to God's Kingdom extended to those outside Israel. This was far beyond the world view of those listening to Jesus at the time and it proved hard for them to grasp. Equally, the parables of the Lost Sheep, Coin and Son (Luke 15) told in the presence of 'tax collectors and sinners' along with the complaining and antagonistic voices of the Pharisees reveal the extent of the grace and salvation of God. For those who had ears to hear this was Jesus telling stories in order to revolutionize the common conceptions of what God's Kingdom was thought to be.

1.7   Imagination can exert negative images or influence as well as positive. How we imagine mission is closely connected with the outworking of mission. It is shaped in the practical realities of what is possible in particular contexts. Another way of thinking about the mission imagination is to use the word 'vision'. How we envision mission can either limit what we engage in practically or it can expand the possibilities we perceive. These can be described as different narratives of mission. In the post-colonial era (post 1950s) Christian world mission in some places became a negative word conjuring up images of proselytism and exploitation while mission in England was not considered to be mission at all. It was thought that as a Christian country England didn't need mission as English culture had been influenced by Christianity over many centuries and the majority of the population saw themselves as 'Church of England'. Much has changed. The Church of England has been re-imagining mission at many levels for some years as the place of the Church of England in English society has changed. We now live in a culture or cultures where Christian faith is not the only language for religion or spirituality. These dilemmas are faced by Christians of every denomination and all churches can learn from each other.

1.8   To see the nature of how the mission imagination or narrative has changed, it is necessary to look briefly at history. For the nineteenth-century Victorian church its mission imagination was about sending missionaries to countries that did not know Christian civilization. It was about imparting something of us to them. It was a confident age that understood its role in the world as one of superiority in religion and culture. It was a time of large vision fuelled by technological and economic progress which was exported to a supposedly needy and less advanced world.[7]

---

7 Foreign missions were often viewed separately from home missions by those who were less involved in them but not by the founders of such missions. The work of the Clapham Sect and the Oxford Movement, to name but two, is witness to this fact.

1.9   The evangelical revival inspired a large and expansive vision of mission as many Christians sought to express their faith at home and overseas. It was this context that saw the birth of many of the Anglican Mission Agencies though some had already been working for many years.[8] Many Christians gave their lives in the course of exercising sacrificial service on the mission fields as they were then understood. Their service expressed love of God and neighbour. However, such service sometimes had unintended consequences as the presence of a dominant foreign power resulted in social disruption.

1.10   The twentieth century after World War I saw a drastic change in how the church imagined mission. The 1910 World Mission Conference in Edinburgh can be interpreted as the height of Western missionary confidence with its belief in the possibility of reaching the whole world for Christ in their generation. However, the Western world post-1918 saw its moral foundation diminish rapidly. The systematic brutality of battle caused many to question their previous confidence in Western civilization and to re-assess the nature of sin and evil. The middle of the century saw the end of World War II and colonial rule by the Western nations. These changes in the social and political realm brought a time of significant questioning about the role of the Western churches in world mission.

1.11   In the Church of England, which claims to value diversity as part of its identity, there are many differing ways in which mission is imagined and of what it means to be faithful to the gospel. There are other ways in which imagining mission differs. For example, the place of the church building as a tool in mission, the nature and practice of worship and the role of the evangelist to name a few. What is important is to acknowledge that how mission is imagined affects the way it is expressed practically.

1.12   The current context in twenty-first-century Britain is complex and challenging. The Church of England together with its ecumenical partners is discovering the language and practice of mission and evangelism anew. For the Church of England, it is searching to interpret and express them as English Anglicans in the mission contexts of today.

What is shaping the mission imagination today?

1.13 World Christianity

The shape of world Christianity is changing. The centre of Christianity is shifting from the West to the Majority World[9] in the East, to Africa, Latin America and Asia. It is more accurate to say that the future of Christianity will have multiple centres of Christianity. It is in the churches of the Majority World that growth is being experienced at a phenomenal rate. The Pentecostal Churches are popular and are growing fast. A significant development globally has been the emergence of theologies of the Spirit as agent in mission.[10] The Christianities of the Majority World are diverse and culturally distinct – just as Western Christianity is culturally distinct. The churches in the North and West will continue but in increasingly diverse forms. The churches in the different

---

8 The Society for the Promotion of Christian Knowledge and the Society for the Propagation of the Gospel had been established in 1698 and 1701 respectively.

9 The term 'Majority World' is used in preference to Global South or Third World because most of the materially poor people of the world live in the continents of Asia, Africa and Latin America and this term does not imply inferiority as the term 'Third World' had tended to do.

10 See Kim, *Joining in with the Spirit, Connecting World Church and Local Mission*, Epworth, 2009.

global regions will no longer resemble the churches of the West. This is to be warmly welcomed as the churches throughout the world express Christian faith in ways that are culturally appropriate and relevant. Relationships between the churches of the Majority World and the West will be as important as ever, if not more so, and historic relationships will undergo sometimes painful re-evaluation. This is an Ephesian Moment[11] when the old forms of the historic churches of the West live together with the new and emerging Christianities of the Majority World. It is increasingly evident that changes in the world economic order will influence patterns of mission in the future. The growing economic significance of China, India and Brazil, for example, will have a considerable effect on patterns of world mission movements and partnerships. The presence of large numbers of women and young people in the churches of the Majority World has the effect of embedding them into serving local communities and future generations.

1.14   Most significantly, world Christianity lives in an inter-religious global context which is increasingly political in its outworking. This has highlighted the particular tensions that face Christians who live as a minority faith in complex inter-religious contexts. It has also highlighted the importance of inter-religious dialogue as an aspect of relationships across cultures. Here the concept of mission is highly problematic where conversion can be forbidden by law and communicating Christ's gospel is limited or even prohibited. It has also highlighted the fact that relationships in one part of the world affect those in other parts within very short time periods. The post-9/11 world has brought inter-religious dialogue to the top of the world mission agenda.

1.15 The Church of England

In the Church of England many parish churches are actively reorientating their priorities to a mission focus and this is bearing fruit both in the depth of spiritual life and in numbers involved in churches. This is also the case ecumenically as all denominations in Britain reorient their lives and priorities towards participating in God's mission in the world. However, there is still a journey to make. In the Church of England the mission imagination of many, but by no means all, parish churches primarily concerns survival. The demands of expensive church buildings as well as the need to pay the quota to the diocese continue to put pressure on parish churches to draw inwards or to see those outside the church as a source of income and funds rather than those who God loves and for whom the church exists. In many places it is not that parish churches do not want to think creatively about mission. Rather it is that the necessity of upkeep of buildings and ministry saps creative thinking. For many, inside and outside our parish churches, the church building exerts a power and influence over memory and association which can lead to tension as important landmarks change and are even threatened. Mission for the Church of England has been a synthesis between parish or community, church building and ministry, largely but not exclusively by the clergy-in-parish model. This way of imagining mission in the local context has proved to be remarkably resilient. It has allowed for variations – for example, church planting, team and group ministries, local ministry teams but has not fundamentally changed. The Decade of Evangelism saw attempts to re-shape these relationships with Robert Warren's work on *Building Missionary Congregations*.[12] This analysis advocated the move from 'Maintenance to Mission' and urged Anglican Christians to imagine their life in new ways based on God's mission in the world.

---

11 A concept developed by Andrew Walls which is based on the cultural context of the Epistle to the Ephesians which describes the short time in the first century when the two Christian cultures, Jewish and Hellenistic, came together. See n. 4 above.
12 Warren, *Building Missionary Congregations*, Church House Publishing, 1994.

Mission-shaped Church

1.16   The publication of *Mission-shaped Church* in 2004 was highly significant in shaping how the Church of England imagines mission in two areas. First, it acknowledged that the parochial system was

> 'no longer able fully to deliver its underlying mission purpose. We need to recognize that a variety of integrated missionary approaches is required.'[13]

Secondly, it advocated that the Church of England is itself now a church in mission and that to be effective witnesses to Christ's love Christians need to cross cultures in our own context. In particular it articulated the nature of changing communities in England based on network rather than geography and how personal and cultural identity is being shaped by these changes. The report relates this to a post-Christendom context where the gulf between Christian faith, the church and cultural context is growing and how the church needs new ways of relating to its context. In essence this would mean adapting to a missionary strategy which focused on telling the story of Jesus within a culture that was in the process of forgetting that story, or for many, hearing it as a new story. This was a new understanding of incarnational mission – not only confined to the parish model but a diversification of that strategy into new worship styles and forms of church. *Mission-shaped Church* gave rise to the movement called Fresh Expressions. Fresh Expressions has led the way in expanding the mission imagination into new ways of being church and of relating to the contemporary context. Fresh Expressions has opened new possibilities for following God in mission in the world.

1.17   With the emphasis on the need to work cross-culturally in the English context Fresh Expressions has also assisted in the breaking down of the division between home and overseas mission. Where home and overseas mission were previously seen as separate categories, it is now the case that differences can be distinguished between them but in essence mission from everywhere to everywhere is cross-cultural. This is reflected in the work of the Mission Agencies. The Church Mission Society (CMS) is heavily involved in Fresh Expressions and in pioneer minister training and has mission partners in the UK involved in Fresh Expressions as well as in the wider world. Equally, the Church Army was heavily involved in the process that led to the publication of *Mission-shaped Church* and is central to the continuing development and vision of Fresh Expressions.

1.18   In highlighting the role of the Mission Agencies in Fresh Expressions, the influence and contribution of the voluntary society to God's mission can be seen. The interaction of voluntary society and church structures is an example of the principles of the two structures of modality ('the structured fellowship') and sodality (a structured fellowship where there is a conscious decision to join beyond the modality structure) as developed by Ralph Winter.[14] The modal is the Church of England structures and the sodality is the Mission Agencies and the Religious Communities for example. The relationship between these two structures of being church are interdependent but church as both modality and sodality need each other and each are vital for the life of the other.[15]

---

13 *Mission-shaped Church*, Church House Publishing, 2004, p. x.
14 Winter and Hawthorne (eds), *The Two Structures of God's Redemptive Mission*, Paternoster Press, 1999, pp. 220–9.
15 Extensive work has been done in this area by Dr George Lings of the Church Army.

1.19   Cross-cultural relationships have been part of the life of dioceses and parishes of the Church of England for many years. Whether through supporting the Anglican Mission Agencies or through Diocesan Companion Links there is experience to be shared at all levels of the Church of England on relationships across cultures. What Fresh Expressions challenges and is seeking to enable is the need to transfer this learning and experience into mission in England. However, this is an altogether more difficult process as it requires a complex process of listening and reflection to understand our presuppositions and practices within our own culture. However, listening to the voices of the global church and first generation migrant residents in England can provide valuable insights and ideas as to how we can learn in our own context. The way we think about mission is challenged and, it is hoped, expanded and extended as we listen deeply to the global church and the migrant churches in England. This involves a willingness to be open with others about our vulnerabilities as well as our strengths. However, our world church partners and those arriving in England from other parts of the world have not always found the Church of England open and willing to learn from them. Relationships across cultures can expand our imagination in the service of God's mission in the world as the local church understands itself as part of the global church. There is a blurring of the boundaries between home and overseas mission as new ways of participating in God's mission in the world emerge.

The ecological and environmental crisis

1.20   The ecological and environmental crisis is shaping how we imagine mission. This crisis has caused many in the churches to re-evaluate our understanding of creation and the created order. The fifth Mark of Mission, with its language of 'respect', 'sustain' and 'renew' is playing an important part in this process. There has been a movement in Christian thinking away from the emphasis on 'dominion'[16] to interdependence or interconnectedness as a way of understanding the place of humanity in God's world. While dominion is a fundamental biblical concept that expresses part of the role of humanity in looking after the earth and providing for humanity's needs it is not the same as exploitation of the earth.

> 'Misguided anthropocentrism has had unfortunate effects both on the earth and on humanity itself.'[17]

Interconnectedness or interdependence, however, is a characteristic of the *missio dei*, in that the mission of God in the world ultimately concerns the bringing together or reconciliation of all creation under the Lordship of Christ.[18] This is the redemption of all creation, human and non-human. This is the ultimate end of God's mission in creation. As the Archbishop of Canterbury says,

> 'Creation is an act of communication. It is God expressing his intelligence through every existing thing.'[19]

So, creation is integral to God's mission. Through the environmental crisis and the impact of climate change we are discovering new shapes or rhythms of God's mission.

---

16 Genesis 1.28.
17 *Sharing God's Planet*, Church House Publishing, 2005, GS 1558, p. 21.
18 Ephesians 1.10.
19 *Sharing God's Planet*, p. vii.

1.21 **Mission as reconciliation**

Another way of understanding mission is as reconciliation. God's mission is to bring all things together in and under the Lordship of Christ (Ephesians 1.10) which represents a reconciliation of all things in three directions; between humanity and God, between human communities and between humanity and creation. The recent report *Living Thankfully Before God: Living fairly before each other*[20] argues that thankfulness should form the basis of life lived in the grace of God which leads towards the flourishing of humanity within creation and that, 'the interconnectedness of the world means that we cannot tackle these problems on our own even if we wanted to'.[21] The publication *Unreconciled?*[22] sees Jesus as the midwife of salvation where reconciliation is about the creation of that which is new, something birthed anew rather than just mended.

1.22   There is a practical impact of climate change and environmental crisis on all church partnerships which involves the Companion Links, the Mission Agencies of the Church of England as well as the Development Agencies. The demands on our partnerships are likely to increase rather than decrease as impoverished regions are forced to deal with high food and commodity prices as well as the reduction in land for agricultural use and the corresponding detrimental effect on social and community life. Climate change, the environmental crisis and world mission are intimately connected. The Anglican Alliance for Relief, Advocacy and Development is highlighting food security as a key element in its work. Living responsibly in God's world is becoming a strong theme in personal discipleship and church life as those in the high consumption areas of the West understand the impact of their lifestyle on the Majority World. Partnership will be increasingly expressed in terms of how personal and corporate lifestyle impacts others across cultural and political boundaries. In the West lifestyle changes become an important part of our discipleship because of their impact on Majority World partners.

The Five Marks of Mission

1.23   The Church of England's thinking and practice about mission has been strongly shaped by the Five Marks of Mission.[23] The Five Marks have been used in many dioceses, deaneries and parishes as well as in the Anglican Communion as a significant descriptor of holistic local mission and as a flexible tool for the practice of local and global mission. The Five Marks of Mission have also been used ecumenically by local, regional and national churches. They have given churches a practical language and image of mission that can be applied locally as well as globally. The Five Marks provide a spectrum of understandings of mission that can embrace both evangelism and development and that retain integrity as marks of God's mission in the world. The Five Marks have been used as a benchmark and a guide to being a missionary church. However, the Five Marks are not an exhaustive set of marks of mission and there are further issues to be considered. The Anglican Consultative Council (ACC) is in the process of reviewing the Five Marks of Mission and the following comments from the Church of England are offered to that process.

---

20 June 2010.
21 *Living Thankfully*, House of Bishops, 2010, p. 23.
22 Anne Richards with the Mission Theology Advisory Group, CTBI, 2011.
23 The Five Marks of Mission originated from the Anglican Consultative Council (ACC 6), 1984, *Bonds of Affection*, p. 49.

1.24   First, the Five Marks are 'marks' but it is not defined theologically what those marks express. The Five Marks of Mission are characteristics of God's mission in the world and are signs of God's gracious and generous presence in his world building the Kingdom of justice and peace in Christ. The roots of the Five Marks of Mission are in God's mission as it is God who is the initiator in mission out of love for the world as an overflowing movement from the communion of the Trinity. Each of the Marks is an expression of God's overflow of love into the world and where they are evident they are a mark or sign of God's mission.

1.25   A suggested change to the Five Marks concerns the primacy of the first mark of mission.

'To proclaim the good news of the Kingdom.'

It is proposed that as this first mark of mission embraces all of the other four marks it should be the key statement about everything in mission. It expresses what Jesus himself says about his nature and mission. While this is a welcome development it should not mean that the evangelistic element in this statement be lost in a more general interpretation. The proclamation of the good news of God's Kingdom is that to which all other activities are purposed.

1.26   Worship and mission go together in an Anglican understanding of mission. The celebration in word and sacrament of God's love and goodness is at the heart of all mission activity not as a spur to mission but as the heart of mission itself. The heart of mission is encounter with God and the expression of that encounter in the complexities of the world. This in turn leads to the church living as a mission community focused on God's activity in the world. It is argued that this aspect of mission be included in the Five Marks.[24]

1.27   A fundamental area of mission that is not currently reflected in the Five Marks is reconciliation. It has been noted earlier that reconciliation of all things in Christ is the eschatological hope that God's entire mission in the world points to. Reconciliation is at the heart of God's mission as an immediate reality and as a long-term hope. A world reconciled to and in Christ is what God's Kingdom is like.

1.28   The Five Marks of Mission have been instrumental in shaping the mission imagination of the Church of England. They have been a major instrument in reconciling different views of what constitutes mission. One example of this is the dichotomy between evangelism and social action. Through their profound simplicity they have helped the church at all levels to hold together different expressions of mission and at the same time seeing each mark as part of a whole.

1.29   The Five Marks are being used to shape perceptions of what mission means for new generations of younger Christians who are exploring and finding their vocation in taking part in God's mission. Whether as a foundation in study courses or exploring Christianity more generally, the Five Marks offer a simple but not simplistic set of images of God at work in the world and the many ways in which younger as well as older Christians are called to serve. The Anglican Communion is in the process of publishing a book by young people on the Five Marks of Mission following the Edinburgh 2010 World Mission Conference 'Witnessing to Christ Today'.

1.30   The role of young people participating in God's mission is vital for the future of the Church of England and the Anglican Communion. Young people are increasingly becoming the leaders in participating in mission through the Mission Agencies, Companion Links, Development Agencies or through parish and higher education links. They are experiencing the breadth and diversity of the world and church in numbers previously unimaginable through short-term visits.

---

24 For a discussion of mission and worship see *Presence and Prophecy*, Chapter 10, p. 133.

The Church of England needs this experience to be held and heard at the centre of its life and throughout its structures.

Integral mission and holistic mission

1.31   An influential and helpful way of describing God's mission in the world is known as Integral Mission. Originating in Latin American evangelical mission theology in the 1980s it holds as its centre the belief that

> 'Integral mission or holistic transformation is the proclamation and demonstration of the gospel. It is not simply that evangelism and social involvement are to be done alongside each other. Rather, in integral mission our proclamation has social consequences as we call people to love and repentance in all areas of life. And our social involvement has evangelistic consequences as we bear witness to the transforming grace of Jesus Christ. If we ignore the world we betray the word of God which sends us out to serve the world. If we ignore the word of God we have nothing to bring to the world. Justice and justification by faith, worship and political action, the spiritual and the material, personal change and structural change belong together. As in the life of Jesus, being, doing and saying are at the heart of our integral task.'[25]

1.32   This framework or lens for understanding and expressing God's mission in the world focuses on moving beyond previous dichotomies in an evangelical understanding of mission such as whether evangelism or social action should take precedence. The Micah Declaration envisages evangelism and social action as being one in God's mission though with different practical expressions. As the Cape Town Commitment states,[26]

> 'Integral mission means discerning, proclaiming, and living out, the biblical truth that the gospel is God's good news, through the cross and resurrection of Jesus Christ, for individual persons, *and* for society, *and* for creation. All three are broken and suffering because of sin; all three are included in the redeeming love and mission of God; all three must be part of the comprehensive mission of God's people.'

1.33   While Integral Mission represents a significant attempt to overcome and unite certain polarizations within an evangelical understanding of mission it has value within other areas of the mission of the church. It is representative of the nature of mission discourse that seeks to unite differing understandings or lenses rather than polarize – a notable characteristic of current mission theology and a welcome rhythm to the theme. One example is the differing approaches between mission and development which will be discussed in a later chapter.

1.34   Today the mission imagination emerging from Anglican, ecumenical and evangelical spirituality shows a distinct movement towards integration, wholeness and embracing what were previously divided understandings such as evangelism and social action. A search for continuity, wholeness and togetherness is happening despite the existence of issues which divide sharply. Integration rather than polarization in God's mission in the world is an evident trend. The search is for frameworks that unite in understanding mission rather than debates about a single definition of mission. Wholeness and integration are becoming the common elements of such a framework.

---

25 The Micah Declaration on Integral Mission, www.micahnetwork.org.
26 The Commitment agreed at the Cape Town 2010 Lausanne Congress on World Evangelization Conference, October 2010.

Conclusion

1.35   Having briefly reviewed the movements and rhythms of God's mission in recent history it is time to ask: How might we imagine the participation of the Church of England in God's mission in the future? In other words, what are the next steps on the journey? Where is God calling the Church of England, together with other churches in the West, to change and what to sustain from our histories? What is it that God is calling to change and renew? The future foundation of the Church of England's participation in God's mission will be a renewed confidence in the local mission of the parish as it has been historically understood as presence in local communities throughout England. At the heart of such local presence will be the faithful proclamation of the Kingdom of God through worship through which it engages in the world and its prophetic pointing to new ways of living. Fundamental to this will be the confidence of new generations of young people taking their place in God's mission. It will be a new awareness that the local church can only find its vocation in connection with the global mission of God. Local will find connection with the global in joy and in suffering as each stands alongside the other. All of this can only be realized through the vulnerability, sacrifice and service of the incarnate one – Jesus Christ. This will mean playing a new tune, a new rhythm with its roots in the mission of God which is always new, always moving and always at work. It will mean taking part in the infinite and surprising nature of God's Spirit at work in the world.

Chapter 2

Partnership, Participation and Hospitality

Summary

This chapter describes the emergence of partnership as a concept in mission discourse and critiques its use. It highlights the relationship between partnership and *missio dei* and argues that partnership needs development and refreshing if it is to provide a mission theology for today. Participation and hospitality are suggested as conceptual developments that enhance partnership.

Introduction

2.1 The governing principle for the Church of England concerning world mission relationships since the mid-1960s has been partnership. While this concept has opened up possibilities for new shapes of relationships in the immediate post-colonial social climate, it has also proved to be difficult to grasp and implement as relationships have progressed. This chapter will explore the theology of partnership and how partnership has been exercised in and through the Mission Agencies and the Diocesan Companion Links. It will assess the benefits of this approach as well as outlining its enduring challenges. It will argue that partnership needs further articulation and the adoption of a deeper level of understanding and practice through concepts such as participation and hospitality. While not rejecting partnership, it will be argued that this was essentially a language of the post-colonial era and a new language for new times is needed. The language of mission today is often expressed in terms of 'community', 'relationship' and 'encounter'. These represent a wider understanding of mission beyond the more formal understandings of partnership.

2.2 Partnership is a multi-faceted concept that is difficult to define with any accuracy. The Oxford English Dictionary definition of partner is

> 'a person who takes on an undertaking with another or others especially in a business or firm with shared risks and profits'.[27]

Partnership holds notions both of difference and shared concerns. It implies a coming together of people of difference in a shared enterprise. One of the most common uses of the word is with business relationships involving financial arrangements. For example, a partner in a firm of solicitors or accountants has reached a level of seniority that involves a substantial level of ownership. Likewise a product may be produced 'in partnership with'. The term 'partner' also works in modern usage to denote a relationship of intimacy and depth that does not have the

---

27 OED, www.oxforddictionaries.com.

14

legally binding nature of marriage. Partnership is a word or concept denoting a closeness of working together that entails some element of commitment even if this is only aspirational. Another example would be the use of the word to describe the need for greater joint working between the National Health Service and Social Services in England. A new partnership is hailed as a deepening in working relationships that can be represented by a Memorandum of Understanding or working agreement. To summarize: one prominent missiologist has described the word 'partnership' as

> 'this deceptively simple term masks a complex reality'.[28]

2.3   Partnership in the context of the Christian faith is a deeper expression of relationship involving relationship with the Trinitarian God and each other. It also reflects the nature of God as Three in One. The biblical word used to denote partnership is *koinonia* translated partnership or communion. Another term closely related to partnership is companion. Dioceses have 'Companion Links' not partnership links. This has a strong sense of those who eat bread together, which includes encounter, friendship and mutuality rooted in a eucharistic relationship.

History of partnership in the Anglican Communion and the Church of England

2.4   The history of the concept of partnership in theological and ecclesial use can be traced back to the Edinburgh 1910 World Mission Conference. It was the young Anglican priest from India, the Revd V. S. Azariah who stated in an impassioned speech,

> 'The exceeding riches of the glory of Christ can be fully realized not by the Englishman, the American and the Continental alone, nor by the Japanese, the Chinese and the Indians by themselves – but by all working together, worshipping together and learning together the Perfect Image of our Lord and Christ, it is only "with all the Saints" that we can "comprehend the love of Christ which passeth knowledge, that we might be filled with all the fullness of God … We ought to be willing to learn from one another and to help one another.
>
> Through all the ages to come the Indian church will rise up in gratitude to attest the heroism and self-denying labours of the missionary body. You have given your goods to feed the poor. You have given your bodies to be burned. We also ask for love. Give us friends!'[29]

This extensive quotation summarizes the essence of partnership in the Christian sense – being together under the Lordship of Christ – even though the word was not used at this time. It highlights one of the essential characteristics of equal partnership – friendship.

2.5   The word partnership can be identified first in ecumenical discussions on world mission before it emerged in Anglican discourse. The term 'partnership' emerged into the foreground of mission thinking as 'partners in obedience' at the 1947 Conference of the International Missionary Conference at Whitby, Ontario, Canada. While the issue of mission relationships had long been on the agenda of previous mission conferences of the International Missionary Council in Jerusalem and Tambaram it was at Whitby that the concept of partnership began to take shape. Some of the key issues concerned the relationship of the younger and older churches and how

---

28 Bonk, Editorial, *International Bulletin of Missionary Research*, vol. 34, no. 3, July 2010, p. 1.
29 Azariah quoted by Stanley in *The World Missionary Conference, Edinburgh 1910*, Eerdmans, p. 125.

and when autonomy in governance could be given to the younger churches. This was heightened by the early independence movements particularly in India. Canon Max Warren, then General Secretary of the Church Missionary Society, attended the Whitby meeting where he led the worship and where it is likely that discussions contributed to his thinking about partnership which found expression in his 1955 book entitled *Partnership*. This short but important book has had greater effect on partnership thinking than any official church report and is widely acknowledged as a formative text. Attention will be given to it in the theological section of this chapter.

2.6   In Anglican thinking partnership emerged at the 1963 Third Congress of the Anglican Communion held in Toronto. This Congress adopted the highly significant report 'Mutual Responsibility and Interdependence' (MRI) which led to the establishment of the early Companion Links across the Communion. The Missio document *Patterns of International Mission Structures in the Anglican Communion* describes this process,

> 'Since 1963 the Anglican Communion has initiated two Communion-wide programmes to encourage mutual participation and support in the mission of the church – *Mutual Responsibility and Interdependence (MRI)* and *Partners in Mission (PIM)*.

The Communion as a whole began its journey from paternalism to partnership in its mission relations in the 1960s. In 1963, just prior to the Anglican Congress in Toronto, the Primates and Metropolitans of the Communion issued a 'manifesto' entitled *Mutual Responsibility and Interdependence in the Body of Christ – MRI*. Their proposal was essentially to look at needs (for people, finance, skills and infrastructure) across the Communion and to gather and distribute resources to meet those needs. It was a challenge to break out of the donor/recipient mindset of the colonial era and move into new relationships of equality and mutuality, not just in financial sharing but in personnel and other aspects of Christian discipleship. A call was made for a fund of five million pounds to assist the new provinces. A priority was theological education to encourage self-reliance in leadership. MRI increased awareness of the Communion, the need for partnership, and the principles on which it should be based. The final part of the manifesto reads as follows:

> We are aware that such a programme as we propose, if it is seen in its true size and accepted, will mean the death of much that is familiar about our churches now. It will mean radical change in our priorities – even leading us to share with others as much as we spend on ourselves. It means the death of old isolations and inherited attitudes. It means a willingness to forgo many desirable things, in every church.
>
> In substance what we are really asking is the rebirth of the Anglican Communion, which means the death of many old things but – infinitely more – the birth of entirely new relationships. We regard this as the essential task before the churches of the Anglican Communion now.[30]

2.7   The movement from 'paternalism to partnership' is indicative of the contemporary political situation where the rejection of colonial government and structures gave rise to new forms of indigenous government. The Anglican Communion had spread with the presence of British influence in its various forms and had been part of British exports abroad. In the light of this new ways of understanding relationships between churches needed to be explored.'

---

30 From *Patterns of Inter-Communion Mission Relationships*, Missio, www.anglicancommunion.org.uk/ missio.

2.8   Apart from the development of the Companion Links, the Mutual Responsibility and Interdependence document gave rise to the Communion-wide process Partners in Mission. The purpose of PIM was to engage the churches of the Communion in a process of setting its mission priorities in which process they would be accompanied by partner churches selected by the host church. The Church of England took part in this process in 1981. The effect of the PIM Consultation upon the Church of England was marginal. The process included a debate in General Synod where Standing Orders were suspended and while many appreciative comments were made on the contributions of the external partners, there was no real process established for the integration of the ideas generated to become part of the lifeblood of the Church of England. The General Synod debate reveals that, at times, the process was difficult and painful for those from the Church of England[31] and the central message of the external partners was that it lacked a vitality of vision for the gospel. Salient points were also raised about the lack of partnership working between the voluntary agencies and the central structures of the Church of England and about the number of voluntary agencies working in world mission though the newly established Partnership for World Mission was applauded by the external partners as a necessary and welcome development. Reading the General Synod debate 29 years later showed its prophetic nature. Many of the things regarding the need for mission to form the life of the Church of England have, or are being, fulfilled. However, there seems to be little evidence of a process to assess and receive what was brought to the Church of England from its external partners. As Philip Groves concludes on the PIM process as a whole,

> 'there was as clear a distinction between giving and receiving churches at the end of the process as at the beginning. The giving churches were offered the chance to receive but were unable or unwilling to do so. The churches regarded as receiving had little opportunity to offer themselves to the younger churches and the giving church did not value their resources.'[32]

2.9   In effect the PIM process did not impact the Church of England to any significant degree and an opportunity was missed. The Revd Canon Humphrey Taylor, then General Secretary of USPG, described the process at the 1986 Mission Agencies Conference,

> 'The Church of England still has no formal mechanism whereby General Synod members who have represented it at PIM Consultations elsewhere can report back to it, let alone allowing external partners to contribute to its own deliberations ... After the external partners, politely heard or even treated like oracles, have departed, the Church carries on its business much as it did before.'[33]

2.10   Since 1986 mechanisms have been put in place for a stronger relationship between the Mission Agencies and the central structures of the Church of England. Just prior to the PIM process in 1981 came the establishment of Partnership for World Mission (PWM) in 1978 which provided such a loose structure established in line with the Partners in Mission process. The Working Party which recommended the establishment of PWM said,

> 'For the first time in the area of world mission, which includes the church in England as much as the church in other lands, there would exist a specific co-ordinating organ for

---

31 See the speech of Canon Colin Craston, *Partners in Mission Presentation*, July 1981, York GS Misc 151, p. 6. The Report of the PIM process in the Church of England is entitled *To A Rebellious House*, CIO, 1981.
32 Philip Groves, unpublished PhD thesis, p. 92.
33 *Progress in Partnership, Report of the Mission Agencies' Conference,* Anglican Consultative Council, 1987, p. 79.

mission to which all the parties involve can relate in a way which visibly demonstrates the Church of England's determination to play her share in the world task.'[34]

2.11　Such a body as PWM was designed to bridge the gap between the central structures and the Mission Agencies and, it was hoped, would bring world mission closer to the central decision-making structures. It was hoped that through PWM there would be a strengthening of relationships and partnership between the synodical structure including the House of Bishops, the Mission Agencies and the dioceses. Such partnership was necessary at home as well as between partner churches in the world church.

2.12　Partnership in World Mission has continued to exercise these functions under four secretaries and now under the World Mission Policy Adviser as it faces another period of transition and development. One of the most significant events of its life was the signing of the Covenant for Common Mission and Co-operation by all the General Secretaries of the Mission Agencies in 2003. The governing body of PWM is now the World Mission and Anglican Communion Panel which brings together representatives of the Mission Agencies, the Companion Links, representatives of the Archbishops of Canterbury and York, the Anglican Consultative Council, the network of Diocesan Development Advisers and the General Synod under an Episcopal Chair appointed by the Archbishops of Canterbury and York. The Panel takes responsibility through the Secretary of PWM for the Annual World Mission Conference. Beginning its life as a Diocesan Companion Links Conference, it is now emerging as the central point at which all the various components of the Church of England's relationships in world mission come together. An essential part of that process is hearing and receiving from our partners from the global church.

2.13　Apart from Partners in Mission the other Communion-wide initiative was the Decade of Evangelism called for by the 1998 Lambeth Conference following an initiative of His Holiness John Paul II. While the Decade had many detractors, what it did was to focus the Anglican Communion on the essential nature of evangelism in God's Kingdom. For many of the churches in the global north, including the Church of England, it was a call to recover the energy, life and vitality of the gospel that was all too evident in the churches of the South. Though its outcomes were limited it raised questions in the Church of England about its lack of zeal for evangelism and at parish level it encouraged many Christians to engage with and explore their faith through courses such as Alpha, Emmaus and others. The hallmark of the Decade in the Church of England became 'from maintenance to mission'. The Anglican Communion joined together at the Kanuga Conference in 1995 to mark the Mid-term of the Decade of Evangelism where it affirmed the distinctive contribution of Anglicans to evangelism as respectful listening and proclamation within the context of incarnational presence and pastoral care.[35]

2.14　In 2006 the Inter-Anglican Standing Commission on Mission and Evangelism published its report entitled *Communion in Mission*.[36] In reviewing current trends and developments in Anglican world mission it picks up a number of themes raised in the 1999 report of Missio[37] notably questions surrounding the use of the word 'partnership'. This had been brought into sharp focus by the vastly changed situation where the growing churches in the Communion are in the

---

34 *Partnership for World Mission, Report of the Working Party on Relations between the Church of England, the General Synod and the Missionary Societies*, CIO, 1977, p. 28.

35 See *G-Code 2000, Report of the Mid-term of the Decade of Evangelism Conference*, Kanuga, Anglican Communion Office, 1996.

36 Anglican Communion Office, 2006, pp. 44–50.

37 *Patterns of International Mission Structures in the Anglican Communion*, ACO, 1999.

global South, and were showing a life and vitality quite alien to the churches in the North. It was also recognized that it was all too easy for partnership to fall quickly into old patterns of the colonial mindset. Missio suggests the movement from the use of the word 'partnership' to 'companionship' as they had noticed a

> 'significant narrowing of the meaning of the term partnership in the 1990s. The word is increasingly used to describe specific programmes or collaborative activity between agencies or diocese'.[38]

Companionship, they advocate, better describes a broader relationship of trust, listening and learning.

2.15   The 2006 report calls the churches of the Communion to deepen their understanding of partnership and to adopt a new or alternative word for the relationships that go across cultural boundaries. The report also suggests 'companion' as well as 'Brother-Sister' and 'friend'. There is also the word 'hospitality'.

2.16   This brief historical summary has focused on the development of the idea of partnership in the Ecumenical Councils and the Anglican Communion and how that impacted the Church of England. This part of the story reveals how a movement or weaving of ideas across Councils and Communion has brought the idea of partnership into the workings of the Church of England and how such bodies can assist the churches as a whole to critique and develop their common life as the worldwide Body of Christ. There is interconnectedness as the churches search for unity in their common mission in the world expressed with different emphases but each needing the other. It raises the question 'whither partnership?' What is the future for this idea that Warren described as

> 'an idea whose time has not yet fully come'?[39]

Is the Church of England now called to look at partnership in a different way? Can she move from being predominantly the giver to become the receiver as the changing shape of the Anglican Communion shows growth and vitality in the continents of Africa, Asia and Latin America rather than the North and West? How the Church of England receives the gifts of the world church has been a common focus of discussion in mission discourse for many years. Does there need to be an assessment of current practices in world mission concerning the giving of money? When large amounts of money pass from the Church of England to our partners in other parts of the global church whose needs are being met? How do we build relationships of equal partnership or, to use a well-used phrase, 'mutual responsibility and interdependence'? Does there need to be a change in the way we use language to describe world mission? Or will this merely mask the subtle but significant changes in attitude that need to occur at a deeper level? These, and other questions, will form the basis of this discussion for the development of world mission in the Church of England. The overall aim is to ask how we can deepen our understanding and practice of partnership for the sake of God's Kingdom in God's world today.

---

38 *Patterns of International Mission Structures in the Anglican Communion*, p. 12.
39 Warren, *Partnership*, SCM Press, 1956, p. 11.

Theology of partnership

Partnership and the *missio dei*

2.17   The most significant development in mission theology in the second half of the twentieth century was the emergence of the concept of the missio dei, the mission of God. The *missio dei* emphasizes that the origin of mission is found in the God the Holy Trinity. This was a significant movement away from the understanding of mission as the task of the church. God the Trinity is the one who sends the church (John 20.21). Mission is the expression of God's unfolding purposes as they reveal God's nature and purpose. God's church is sent following in the way of Christ and as sign and foretaste of the Kingdom. The role of the church is to discern where God is at work and to follow in obedience. Hartenstein as one of the earliest commentators on the *missio dei* said,

> 'mission is not just the conversion of the individual, not just obedience to the world of the Lord, nor just the obligation to gather the church. It is the taking part in the sending of the Son, the missio dei, with the holistic aim of establishing Christ's rule over all redeemed creation.'[40]

2.18   The phrase *missio dei* was first adopted at the 1952 International Missionary Council Conference in Willingen, Germany. With this re-orientation of mission as a movement from God to the world came a re-orientation of the place of the church and the Kingdom of God. The church-centred mission that focused its main strategy on church planting and social provision of education and medicine became a limited understanding. Once the Triune God became the origin, source and primary actor in mission then the world took on a different perspective. The Kingdom of God came to be understood as bigger and beyond the church but which involved the church as sign, instrument and foretaste of the Kingdom.

2.19   What of the relationship between *missio dei* and partnership? The emergence of the two concepts so closely together at the 1947 Whitby Conference and at the 1952 Willingen Conference show a convergence of ideas at something of a *kairos*[41] moment in mission history. Wider political changes taking place in the 1950s necessitated the re-thinking of old patterns of working in mission and the articulation of new theory and practice. The expulsion of the missionaries from China, which had been one of the largest of the mission fields, had occurred between 1949 and 1951 and this sent shock waves through the Mission Agencies, the churches and conciliar ecumenism. While partnership was the new articulation of the relationships between sending and receiving churches and other forms of missionary engagement, so *missio dei* was the articulation of a new theological understanding of the church in mission in relationship with the Trinitarian God and the God's Kingdom.

2.20   Theologically the two concepts interweave and interrelate. Ross argues that, 'partnership is an idea essential to the very nature of God ... we see partnership in the Godhead ... God is a community of three divine persons. God is also one God'.[42] God is not self-contained but has, by God's nature and love, to express personally and reach beyond itself. Mission is the self-expression of God for God's creation or, as Bosch describes the Trinity,

> 'a fountain of sending love'.[43]

---

40 Hartenstein in Freytag (ed.), *Mission zwischen gestern und morgen*, 1952, p. 54.
41 Greek for a significant time of openness to change.
42 Ross, *International Bulletin of Missionary Research*, vol. 34, no. 3, July 2010, p. 145.
43 Bosch, *Transforming Mission*, Orbis, 1991.

2.21   John V. Taylor states, 'Partnership between Churches in mission means also an apostolic concern from one to the other to help one another to present the likeness of Christ more clearly; being in travail for one another until we all are formed in the shape of Christ.'[44]

Has our partnership become too focused on the sharing of resources and in particular giving money rather than 'being in travail' for each other as we are shaped in the likeness of Christ? What would partnership look like if Christ were its focus and its centre? The centrality of Christ as the primary focus of partnership would be marked by a searching for holiness and wholeness with the worship of God at its heart.

2.22   There is a need to re-focus our understanding towards relationships, participating together in the life of God through Christ and the power of the Spirit. Participate becomes the verb to describe our relating as we take part in the aim of all mission which is to

> 'present the person of Jesus Christ, to make *him* visible, to lift *him* up as he truly was and is, so that *he* rather than anything else we bring may draw all to himself'.[45]

This calls for a re-orientation of thinking about mission away from resources and towards the person of Christ and to the eschatological vision when all things will be brought together as one (Ephesians 1.9–10).

2.23   There is a real and radical equality about where we stand as participants in the mission of God or, as Taylor prefers, the mission 'of Christ'.[46] Who are the givers and who are the receivers when we look at global mission through the eyes of the mission of Christ? Who are those who have the riches and who are the poor? Before everything else all of Christ's church and for Anglicans all of the Anglican Communion stands before God the Holy Trinity in worship and humility. For the Church of England the pertinent question is 'if we didn't have our material resources to share with our partners in the world church what would we be bringing to the relationship?'

2.24   John V. Taylor understands the mystery of the human and divine partnership as, 'God chooses not to act solo in relation to the world, but always with and through its creatures. For it has been God's loving purpose from the beginning to raise those creatures to more and more responsible partnership with their Creator.'[47] Jesus Christ is the perfect example of partnership with God and God's human creatures are also called into that relationship of Sonship.

2.25   Likewise, Walter Brueggemann[48] adopts the concept of partnership to describe the relationship between God and humanity. Rejecting the vagueness of New Age understandings of God and also the settledness of God in scholastic understanding, he describes his understanding of God as 'dialogical'. That is, in interaction with partners (Israel, the nations, human persons and creation) 'that always pushes to a new possibility, that makes demands on both parties and that opens up fresh possibilities for the relationship'. While Brueggemann acknowledges the 'accent of finality' that may accompany the divine intervention, there is always, he says, the new text and dialogue that follows. What this brings us to is a clear link between the nature of God in God's interaction with God's partners and how partners conduct their dialogue (or multilogues) in the image of God.

---

44 Taylor, *The Uncancelled Mandate*, Church House Publishing, 1998, p. 10.
45 *The Uncancelled Mandate*, p. 9.
46 *The Uncancelled Mandate*, p. 8.
47 *The Uncancelled Mandate*, p. 13.
48 Brueggemann, *An Unsettling God*, Fortress, 2009, p. 5.

2.26   Partnership in world mission is primarily an expression of the mission of God through the mission of Christ in the world. It is part of a divine engagement with the world and is expressive of our common identity as children of God. It is part of our participation in the life of God in the world today. This carries a strong element of responsibility that each carries for the other in obedience to the example of Christ.

2.27   While partnership was the new articulation of the relationships between sending and receiving churches and other forms of missionary engagement, so *missio dei* was the articulation of a new theological understanding of the church in mission in relationship with God the Holy Trinity as a part but not the totality of the Kingdom.

2.28   Essentially both *missio dei* and partnership attempt to focus the theory and practice of mission on ways of relating that are expressed through mutuality and reciprocity flowing from the Trinitarian Godhead to the world in love and are then expressed between partners in mission. The heart of this partnership is worship of the Trinitarian God by the partners which establishes equality between them. This is supremely so in the Eucharist as the primary practice of partnership.

Andrew Kirk expresses it thus,

> 'partnership is not so much what the church does as what it is'.[49]

2.29   The biblical root of partnership is *koinonia* which has also been translated communion or fellowship. The Epistle to the Philippians is, according to Tom Wright, all about partnership and one of the most important words in Paul's vocabulary.[50] Paul writes from imprisonment to a beloved church of his pain of separation from them and thanking them for their generosity to him. Communion, partnership or *koinonia* here concern the nature of their relationship of which the financial gift is a part rather than a business arrangement. Paul finds in the relationship with the Philippian church a fellowship of suffering as he invites them to understand their sufferings or persecution in the light of his. Cunningham uses *koinonia* to denote his concept of Trinitarian participation which indicates the common root of participation and partnership.[51] Groves, applies partnership to world mission relationships using the Letter to the Philippians and draws out seven marks of partnership which are agreed task, equal status, a common basis of belief, individually united, regular contact, complementary resources and skills and sharing in struggles and victories.[52] The biblical evidence points to the depth of partnership between Paul and all the churches he planted but particularly so with the Philippian church.

The relational turn

2.30   Is world mission concerned with a task or a relationship? The current movement in mission thinking is away from a task-based focus to the primacy of relationship. This has partly developed as a result of the growth of the churches in the world regions formerly viewed as receiving churches and the continuing development of indigenous leadership in those churches. This movement has also been influenced by developments in Trinitarian theology which stress

---

49 Kirk, *What is Mission?*, DLT, 2002, p. 184.
50 Wright, *Paul for Everyone: The Prison Letters*, SPCK, 2002, p. 84.
51 Cunningham, *These Three Are One*, Blackwell, 1998, pp. 165–69.
52 Groves, *Global Partnerships for World Mission*, Grove Pastoral Booklet P106, pp. 15–19.

the nature of the Trinity as relationship and the implications of that for practical theology and church life.[53]

2.31   The evangelical missiologist, Ralph Winter, describes a four-stage process that results in participation as a model of relational mission. He moves from the missionary as 'pioneer' in Stage 1 where a missionary acts as leader in a context where there are few Christians, through the stages of 'parent' and 'partner' to 'participant' where the indigenous church assumes leadership and a mature, equal relationship exists between missionary and indigenous church. It is important to note the characteristics of the 'partner' stage of the relationship. In this model this is a transitional stage where relationships are changing from parent-child to adult-to-adult relationships. It is acknowledged that this is a difficult phase to move from but is essential to the furtherance of God's mission in the world. This model is helpful in describing a progression in mission relationships rather than providing a blueprint but reflects the commonly held view that our current understandings of partnership are not an end but a stage on the journey. Furthermore, it is necessary to continually move forward on in the journey rather than be fixed in one place.

2.32   What the above model does not describe in detail is how these stages are negotiated by the partners. These movements represent a complex process of change in personnel and context as well as theology and spirituality. In the report of the Edinburgh 2010 Study Group entitled 'Forms of Missionary Engagement'[54] this turn to mission as relationship is outlined. The emphasis is placed on human and divine vulnerability as the heart of mission and poses the question as to whether,

> 'In an age when the majority of Christians live in more vulnerable life situations, we ask ourselves whether vulnerability contains the potential, the capacity and power that can be employed for the purposes of mission.'[55]

That question is posed against the theological background of divine vulnerability in the Incarnation where Christ exchanged power for powerlessness.

2.33   The move to participation as a development of the concept of partnership involves an intensification of mission as relationship or friendship and hospitality as the modus operandi of mission. It is the turn from living alongside each other to working face to face. Face-to-face relationship involves an intimacy that exists to a lesser extent in standing alongside. It suggests the intimacy of both shared being and purpose. Likewise it is a participation that involves greater vulnerability as looking into the face of another is both revelatory and humbling. Participation in mission has its roots in the churches' participation in the life of God and there is no participation in mission without participating in God. Cunningham[56] describes participation as one of the Trinitarian virtues, and

> 'It can help us begin to think about what it might mean to dwell in, and be indwelt by, the lives of others.'

He also uses the image of polyphonic music of Trinitarian relationships. Polyphony has any number of component lines of music which may be making different sounds but do not work against the other. This is a prescient image of the church where different tunes may be played but

53 See among others, Fiddes, *Participating in God*, Westminster John Knox, 2000, and Cunningham, *These Three Are One*, Blackwell, 1998.
54 Balia and Kim (eds), *Edinburgh 2010 Witnessing to Christ Today*, vol. 2, pp. 116–47.
55 Balia and Kim, *Edinburgh 2010 Witnessing to Christ Today*, p. 122.
56 Cunningham, *These Three Are One*, p. 165.

remain part of the whole. Unity between participants is a delightful discovery of common roots in the life of the Trinity and with a common awareness of the life of the world in its joy and brokenness.

2.34   Hospitality, as the mutual indwelling one with another, becomes the modus operandi of mission as those in common participation in the life and mission of God meet and receive from each other. Hospitality can be described as the embrace of the other (see Pohl and Volf and Pohl and Heuertz). A popular example of this is the Rublev Icon of the Trinity depicted as the hospitality of Abraham. The three at table have an open space at the front of the icon signifying openness to the other which is the heart of hospitality. The influence of figures such as the late Henri Nouwen[57] who devoted his later ministry to the exercise of hospitality with people with profound learning disabilities has had a significant influence on understanding mission as hospitality.

Hospitality, understood as the embrace of the other, represents a complex process of moving from being stranger to becoming friend. This involves an often unconscious process known as translation. Paul Ricoeur uses the term linguistic hospitality,

> 'linguistic hospitality, then, where the pleasure of dwelling in the other's language is balanced by the pleasure of receiving the foreign word at home, in one's own welcoming house'.[58]

Ricoeur here is writing of the process of translation but, he argues, translation cannot be done except in a relationship where there is vulnerability and a desire to receive the foreign word. Hospitality is an attitude of the heart which is about openness to the other. Here it goes beyond the image of hospitality as welcoming those who are already known and loved to the welcome of the stranger. This mirrors the hospitality of the Trinity as God chooses to open himself to the other through the Incarnation and to subject himself to the created order. It was the powerful, whether religious or political, who were not hospitable to the incarnate Christ while those who were vulnerable had an openness to the presence of the incarnate one in their midst. This is one meaning of the parable of the Great Banquet as a picture of mission where the poor and vulnerable know openness to the Other, in this case God in human form, that the powerful and rich cannot see. As Pohl says,

> 'Jesus, who was dependent on the hospitality of others during much of his earthly sojourn, also served as the gracious host in his words and in his actions.'[59]

Hospitality, as a practice first of the heart and only then of the table, is participative and practical. It is about a generous acknowledgement and meeting of common humanity as well as meeting the needs of humanity, emotional, spiritual and physical, with generosity. As such it mirrors the activity of God towards creation.

The practice of hospitality can be difficult and demanding. Guest and host have different ways of living and being together. Complex cultural conventions shape such encounters which include the way property is treated, meals are taken and gifts are exchanged. Women, often, bear the burden of hospitality which can become a burden as well as a joy. Hospitality is a ministry of sacrificial giving and openness to the other.

---

57 Nouwen, *Reaching Out: The Three Movements of the Spiritual Life*, Image Books, New York, 1975.
58 Paul Ricoeur, *On Translation*, Routledge, 2006, p. 10.
59 Pohl, *Making Room, Recovering Hospitality as a Christian Tradition*, Eerdmans, 1999, p. 5.

2.35   One of the key issues in world mission relationships is the extent of the openness to receive from the other. This is a costly process which means the laying down of power and dominance and adopting the stance of the open listener and learner who also brings something new to every encounter. The Church of England has to ask itself and its partners whether they find it an open listener and learner and to ask how it might move to that attitude of mind as its own mission context demands it.

2.36   In conclusion, what this chapter advocates is a shift and deepening of theological language in order to create the conditions to intensify our world mission relationships. This concerns the enrichment of our current understanding and use of partnership with the concepts of participation and hospitality. This is not an abandonment of partnership but a recognition that the call to the church worldwide is to deepen and intensify relationships across cultures and to see ourselves as one in partnership with and participating in the life of God the Holy Trinity.

Affirmations and commitments

The Church of England affirms:

- With joy, the partnership shared with the Provinces of the Anglican Communion as well as ecumenical partners in the worldwide church.

- The need for the General Synod to strengthen the processes through which it hears from and responds to the voices of the Provinces of the Anglican Communion.

The Church of England is committed to:

- A theological and spiritual journey of intensified relationship with the Provinces of the Anglican Communion and ecumenical partners focusing on mutual participation in God's mission through generous and practical hospitality.

- Listening and learning through world church relationships.

- Being open to hear the voices of the Provinces of the Anglican Communion as they bear upon the life and witness of the Church of England.

Chapter 3

Partnership in Practice

Summary

This chapter explores the different expressions of partnership in and through the life of the Church of England. The description focuses upon the contributions of the Anglican Mission Agencies and the Diocesan Companion Links. It describes the growing complexity of world mission relationships with the development of many smaller agencies and parish-to-parish links. The chapter concludes with recommendations for the future of world mission in the Church of England.

3.1   How is partnership expressed practically in the life of the Church of England? Throughout its history the Church of England has adopted two major routes to express relationships with the Anglican Church in other parts of the Communion. These are through the Mission Agencies, comprised of the ten Mission Agencies which are full members of Partnership for World Mission and the 21 country or approach-specific Associate members of PWM. The other major route is through the Companion Links of the 44 dioceses. The recent story of the Church of England's involvement in world mission is one of increasing diversity and variety in the ways through which it expresses its partnership with churches in the Anglican Communion and with Ecumenical Links. The growth of the Development Agencies such as Christian Aid and Tearfund has played an important part in this emerging picture. A detailed discussion of the relationships between mission and development will appear in a later chapter.

3.2   The central argument of this chapter is that historically the Church of England has understood its involvement in world mission through the Mission Agencies. The emergence of the Diocesan Companion Links as well as an increasing number of parish-to-parish links and smaller agencies focused on mission has created a picture of increased diversity and complexity. The challenge here is to identify how the contribution of these different approaches can be understood and practised as part of a whole even where there are fundamental differences in approach. How can mutual listening and learning happen in the Church of England and with our global partners in the service of God and God's church?

3.3   This chapter will examine these different routes and outline recent developments in an increasingly diverse picture. The role of the Archbishop of Canterbury as Primate of the Church of England and of the Anglican Communion is a vital part of the expressions of these relationships but is not the main focus of this chapter.

Changing shape of mission service

3.4   In 1910 the most common form of world mission was long-term service through one of the Mission Agencies in one of the countries of the British empire. The missionary went to the mission field for life with, perhaps, one or two periods of furlough. In 2010 the most common form of mission service is short-term service through one of the Mission Agencies, Companion Links or small project-based mission organizations for a project of between two weeks to two years. What has brought about this change? Migration and the development of a network of diaspora churches, the vast increase in personal travel and the use of Information Technology have all contributed to changes in the patterns of mission service as the world has seemed to shrink. The growth and development of indigenous churches and local leadership has influenced the shape of mission service as well as the provision of health and education through development programmes.

3.5 A growing factor in patterns of mission service is the movement of missionaries from the Majority World to Europe and the United States. This flow of mission personnel happens through the denominational route whereby ministers from other parts of the Anglican Communion come to England often through a Companion Link or a Mission Agency. A small number of ministers work in the Church of England through this route. The Church of England's Covenant partner, the Methodist Church, has a long history of receiving ministers from other parts of world Methodism. The Scottish Episcopal Church and the Presbyterian and United Churches in Scotland and Wales have also received from their partners in the Global South in this way. Another route for ministers from overseas is through the churches that emerge from diaspora communities which see themselves as living in England in order to proclaim the gospel to a culture that has lost its spiritual roots. There is also the informal route for those who come to England for work but who will often work through a church as an evangelist. These are trends that are growing. How can the Church of England hear their voices and receive from them?

The Mission Agencies

3.6 The changing shape of mission service has had a vast impact on the work of the Mission Agencies and how they are perceived in the Church of England. The active involvement of the Mission Agencies has been at the heart of the life of the Church of England, some for 300 years or more and others for over a century. Their work and witness represents the dedication of many thousands of Christians in their service of God and the world. It is a rich history. Even though methods of missionary engagement have changed and relationships have been re-evaluated nothing should detract from the sacrificial giving that the work of the Mission Agencies represents in many places throughout the world over many years.

3.7 The ten Anglican Mission Agencies which are full members of Partnership for World Mission are:

> Church Mission Society
> Church Army
> Church's Ministry Among Jewish People
> Church Pastoral Aid Society
> Crosslinks
> Intercontinental Church Society
> Mission to Seafarers
> Mothers' Union
> Society for Promoting Christian Knowledge
> United Society for the Propagation of the Gospel

3.8 The first society formed in 1698 was the Society for Promoting Christian Knowledge and in 1701 the United Society for the Propagation of the Gospel (USPG) was formed. Both were established by the Revd Thomas Bray. The initial purpose of USPG was to minister in the new colonies of what became the USA. The foundational Scripture was the Macedonian Call (Acts 16.6–10). In 1963 the Society for the Propagation of the Gospel joined with the Universities' Mission to Central Africa to become USPG. SPCK has always been concerned with Christian education and literature distribution. The Church Mission Society was formed in 1799 with the Clapham Sect at its heart and with three aims being the abolition of the slave trade, social reform at home and world evangelization. CMS merged with Mid-Africa Ministry in the 1990s and with the South American Missionary Society in 2009. Church Pastoral Aid Society was founded in 1836 by prominent Christians, including the pioneering social reformer Lord Shaftesbury. It was established as a Christian response to the massive social change brought about by the Industrial Revolution. The Mission to Seafarers was founded in 1856, but it had its beginnings some years earlier when John Ashley, an Anglican priest, started visiting ships at anchor in the Bristol Channel in 1835. He found no one from the Church had been near them before. He was so moved by their isolation and need that he gave up a secure living to devote his life to serving them. In 1876 the Mothers' Union was founded by Mary Sumner and was to spread across the world with its focus on the enabling of women. Intercontinental Church Society was formed in 1823 with a focus upon ministry and evangelism among English-speaking peoples abroad. Church Army was founded by the Anglican Clergyman Wilson Carlile in 1882 with the aim of reaching ordinary people with the love of God and of equipping lay Christians to share the good news. In 1809 CMJ or Church's Ministry to the Jews was established by Lord Shaftesbury among others to witness to people of Jewish origin. Crosslinks, then the Bible Churchmen's Missionary Society was formed in 1922. It branched away from CMS over issues concerning the authority of the Bible and has exercised committed mission service in the evangelical tradition up to today.

3.9   The pattern of the establishment of the Mission Agencies shows two important features. First, there is a clear pattern that in times of great social change Christians have sought to establish ministries that are concerned with the lives of ordinary people of which a vital component is witness to Jesus Christ. The enormous influence of the Evangelical Revival known as the Great Awakening in the mid-eighteenth century upon the founders of the evangelically based Agencies and their supporters is crucial in this process. Stanley attributes the eighteenth-century missionary movement to the Great Awakening.[60] Seven out of the ten Mission Agencies which are full members of Partnership for World Mission find their origins in the nineteenth century as the Evangelical Revival found its worldwide expression.

3.10   The second aspect of this growth in the number and scope of the Mission Agencies is that they are the expression of the work of pioneers. These founders were people of vision who identified need and responded. Some of the founders were notable lay people such as Lord Shaftesbury and William Wilberforce. Others were ordained, such as Wilson Carlile and the founders of Intercontinental Church Society and Mission to Seafarers. It is this pioneering emphasis that the Agencies have developed and sustained throughout their histories alongside the institutional Church of England which was often resistant to such pioneering work. One of the main features of the work of the Agencies is that they have encouraged the development of ministry and mission for groups excluded from the official ministry of the Church of England – lay people, women and indigenous non-western peoples. This pioneering dimension is still necessary for the Church of England today. The Mission Agencies continue to be at the forefront of pioneering mission both in England and in the wider world.

3.11   Today, in a changed and changing context, where the Mission Agencies are no longer the major mediator in relationships between the Church of England and overseas partners they

---

60 Stanley, *The Bible and the Flag*, Apollos, 1990, p. 59.

continue to provide an important means whereby mission in the Majority World can be enabled and developed alongside the indigenous church. CMS (Britain) has shared its world mission calling by planting other CMSs in former mission regions. This recognizes that there are multiple centres of Christianity all interchanging mission with each other across the world. USPG focuses its support of indigenous churches through the local Diocesan Bishop and focuses on supporting the local church which may or may not involve a mission partner. The Mission Agencies with their focus on mission in England (CPAS and Church Army) together with CMS, USPG and SPCK have played major roles in enabling the Church of England to see itself as a church in contemporary mission contexts and in the development of Fresh Expressions. CMS and Church Army have both taken the route of becoming Acknowledged Communities representing a holistic vision and practice of mission and spirituality together with renewed relationships in the Church of England in terms of Episcopal oversight and accountability. The Mission Agencies have not stood still. Each, in its own way, has sought to re-imagine its future in partnership with the church in England and overseas and has looked to God for new ways of working. This is a continuing and emerging story.

The voluntary principle

3.12   The relationship of the Mission Agencies to the Church of England has been governed by the voluntary principle. The Mission Agencies are voluntary bodies in that they are separately governed and managed from the institutional church but are fully part of the life of the Church of England. The 1994 Report *A Growing Partnership*[61] outlines the essential nature of the voluntary bodies. It traces the root of the concept of the Mission Agencies to the rise of monasticism. These roots continue to be influential in shaping the future of the Mission Agencies represented in the decisions of CMS and Church Army to become Acknowledged Communities. It goes on to describe the 'new expressions of the voluntary principle'[62] in the seventeenth and eighteenth centuries as the possibility for

> 'lay and ordained people in the Church to come together for the fulfilment of specific aims'.

The Report also emphasizes the fact that the Mission Agencies or societies

> 'become an expression of the Church in mission and service'.[63]

Such bodies are essential to the wider church for witness, renewal and the re-energizing of the life of the church generally. On the subject of leadership the 1994 Report sees the role of leadership in the church to the voluntary societies as one of

> 'recognition, facilitation and direction not of control'.[64]

It also outlines the changing relationships between the voluntary Mission Agencies and the national church structures through the establishment of the Central Board of Missions to the Board of Mission to the establishment of Partnership for World Mission in 1978 which was the first direct structural expression of the relationship between the voluntary societies and the General Synod.

---

61 The Church of England and World Mission, Board of Mission of the General Synod.
62 *A Growing Partnership*, p. 2.
63 *A Growing Partnership*, p. 2.
64 *A Growing Partnership*, p. 2.

The voluntary principle from 1994 to today

3.13   Since the 1994 Report the voluntary principle has continued to operate but questions have been raised about its sustainability. At the same time there is no strong call for the Church of England to adopt a unitary system for working in world mission. Attention has rather been focused on how the Mission Agencies and all partners in the Church of England's world mission relationships work together in an increasingly diffuse picture. While financial challenges have changed the shape of the Mission Agencies far bigger challenges in terms of their role and place in the overall picture of world mission relationships and the Church of England have influenced their life heavily. The emergence of the Diocesan Companion Links and lately direct parish-to-parish links within a direct donor-culture that discourages the role of the middle agency has all challenged the Mission Agencies. So too has the rapid growth of the Development or Aid Agencies with their focus on emergency as well as long-term aid. Equally, the impact of the 2008 world financial crisis on investment funds has been considerable.

3.14   The voluntary principle is not only a feature of the life of the Church of England. It finds its expression ecumenically in the great variety of Mission Agencies that find their roots in evangelical spirituality and mission. In the Roman Catholic Church the New Communities[65] such as Community of the Beatitudes, Community of St John and of Christ the Prince of Peace are examples of communities whose life is recognized by the Holy See and which exercise ministry in evangelization and spirituality.

The future of the voluntary principle

3.15   Key questions about the role of the Mission Agencies today involve issues around their viability and sustainability. A number of futures can be imagined. First, that the current picture is maintained and sustained. Second, that Mission Agencies work more closely together either through complete merger or through combining resources including staff and office facilities. Some of the Agencies have explored this route and in some cases merger has happened. Would it be possible for a generalist Agency to combine with a specialist Agency? Key issues would need consideration concerning the maintenance of the specific identity of the work areas of the Agencies against the tendency for larger Agencies to subsume smaller Agencies.

3.16   Third, that serious consideration is given to certain of the Mission Agencies becoming part of the National Church Institutions of the Church of England or a part of the Anglican Communion structures. Is it so important to maintain the voluntary principle at all costs? Have the central church structures changed sufficiently to allow a creative and pioneering element in their midst?

3.17   Fourth, a future can be imagined where effective partnerships develop between the Mission Agencies and the Companion Links that allow for financial support for both approaches. In times of financial stringency when diocesan and Mission Agency staff are being reduced, jointly funded posts could be considered and be of benefit to both.

The key question concerning the future of the Mission Agencies is how far the Church of England wants its Mission Agencies to remain at the heart of its life and if so how will they be funded?

---

65 Communities established after the Second Vatican Council and acknowledged by the Vatican combining ministry in mission, evangelization and spirituality.

The Mission Agencies Covenant

3.18   In 2003 the then 11 full members of Partnership for World Mission signed a Covenant which established a common vision and a series of commitments for the future. The Covenant envisages a Common Future in which the Agencies remain a 'major channel for on-going mission relationships and grassroots initiatives within the Communion' but where 'there are a growing number of public issues and debates where the Agencies need to be more visible and where their contribution needs to be heard'. The Covenant goes on, 'This calls for new ways of working together to speak with one voice and take joint action' and looks for 'closer working between the Archbishop (of Canterbury) and the Agencies'.[66]

3.19   The Common Vision places the Anglican Agencies within the 'holistic and evangelistic' understandings of mission 'within the context of the Five Marks of Mission'. It endorses partnership 'within the fellowship of the worldwide church' as the way of proclaiming the gospel and affirms the voluntary principle 'as a proven model for mobilizing and encouraging effective engagement'.

3.20   The Common Commitment calls for increased co-operation within diversity, for increased mutual support and for intensified relationships between the General Secretaries and the Archbishop of Canterbury, specialist staff of the Agencies and to 'issue agreed public statements, study and promotional materials' (see text of full Covenant in Appendix 2).

3.21   In the years since the Covenant was signed there have been twice-yearly meetings between the General Secretaries of the Agencies as well as an annual meeting with the Archbishop of Canterbury. There have also been meetings between Agency financial officers. The main example of joint promotional and study material has been the annual St Andrew's Day prayer resources produced by PWM for use in parish churches.

3.22   For the future there needs to be joint reflection on the effect of the Covenant and how it has and could enable future working together. The signing of a Covenant suggests relationships that go beyond pragmatic reasons for working together into shared theological understandings of mission and the belief that each of the Agencies is vital to the whole picture and that, in the absence of one, all are impoverished. This is about a common understanding of working interdependently. There is a need for the Agencies to evaluate their working under the Covenant in order to move towards new areas of joint working and with a view to developing the spirit of the Covenant.

Tools developed for enhancing the Anglican–Methodist Covenant may be helpful in this process. Three characteristics of Covenant living identified by the Anglican–Methodist Joint Implementation Commission are:

1. A gracious giving and a grateful receiving.

2. A purpose which lies beyond the covenant relationship.

3. A constancy and mutual cherishing.[67]

The key question for the Agencies in response to the Covenant of Common Mission is: In times of organizational challenge and change what does it mean for us to live in Covenant today? What increased participation are the Mission Agencies called to in these times?

---

66 Common Mission: A Covenant of the Mission Agencies of the Church of England.
67 *Living God's Covenant*, Anglican–Methodist Covenant website.

Companion Links in the Church of England

3.23   All Church of England dioceses have Companion Links with churches in the Anglican Communion as well as Ecumenical Links with churches in Europe. A recent survey of diocesan-level Links has shown that the total number of Companion Links known to PWM totals 87. Most dioceses have more than one Link and some have up to five Links. This does not include the numerous links between parishes and deaneries that grow up out of personal links and friendships or as part of the Diocesan Link. As well as Diocesan Companion Links the Mothers' Union has an extensive and longstanding network of links at diocesan and parish level. This diverse and enriching picture reveals that, together with the Mission Agencies, the Companion Links make the Church of England an active part of the world church with considerable energy and enthusiasm for interacting with the Anglican Communion and with the wider global church. The main impetus for Companion Links came from the process begun in 1963 with the report *Mutual Responsibility and Interdependence in the Body of Christ* and this growth has been rapid. Some of the Companion Links are now continuing to build on histories of three to four decades while others are more recently established and some have come to completion agreed on all sides. In many dioceses the Companion Links are at the centre of the life of the diocese and enrich its life in many and varied ways. They are integral to the life and culture of the diocese. The pre-Lambeth Conference Hospitality Initiatives, for example, are a key point at which relationships are strengthened and intensified.

Regional distribution

3.24   Based on the recent survey figures quoted above, the regional distribution of the Diocesan Companion Links is as follows:

> Africa – 38 in total and broken down by African regions:
>> East Africa – 15, Southern Africa – 10, West Africa – 5, Central Africa – 6, North Africa – 2
>
> Europe – 25 (Ecumenical Links)
> India, Pakistan and Sri Lanka – 11
> Latin America – 3
> Central America and the Caribbean – 2
> USA and Canada – 4
> Middle East – 2
> Far East – 2
> Pacific – 2
> Australia – 1

> (Note: where a diocese has links with a number of dioceses in one country it has been counted as one Link.)

Differing styles of Companion Links

3.25   If each of the Mission Agencies has its own style and approach, then that diversity is equally true of the Companion Links. The Companion Links are essentially about friendship or companionship and this is expressed in a variety of ways of giving and receiving. Prayer forms an essential part of all Links and this is fostered through Diocesan Prayer Diaries and Plans. Prayer and worship are at the heart of Links and this is the most important aspect. Visits are essential to creating and maintaining friendship and this is often where the Link becomes a reality for many people. It is impossible to track all the different types of visit but dioceses have made visits of bishops, ordinands and curates, readers, young people, teachers and clergy among others to their Link dioceses. The majority will experience some element of transformation as a result of undertaking such a visit which brings much benefit to ministry and mission in England. The Companion Links are one way in which the connection between the local and the global is manifested in the Church of England.

3.26   Giving money is both a great gift and a potential hazard in linking. A Link with a diocese in East Africa, for example, is expressed very differently to a Link with a Lutheran Church in Europe. The challenges of linking between a materially well-resourced diocese in England and a materially less well-resourced diocese are many. Some Links do not involve giving financially and Links should not be defined by financial transaction. Other Links see the giving of money as an important part of expressing concern for and solidarity with those with whom they are linked and an expression of their own thankfulness to God for his generosity. To what extent will these material differences distort the understanding of giving and receiving? How does the English partner guard against old colonial patterns of power and control? What is the place of money in partnerships and how does it enable all parties to participate in God's mission? Links with European churches, where material disparity is not so evident, rest on other ways of giving and receiving. Where is the discussion between different types of Link that can assist each to share their insights and develop practice? It is the case that in many dioceses which have a number of Companion Links in various global regions different office holders take responsibility for the Links which can result in a lack of learning between Links.

3.27   Some Companion Links are time-limited and others are continuous. Initially it was advised that Links should be time-limited but general experience has shown that to provide for a process of regular evaluation and review and an understanding that the Link can be terminated is more important.

What is the purpose of Companion Links?

3.28   The 2001 PWM document, '*Living Links*',[68] cites six reasons for having a Companion Link using material originating from Lichfield Diocese:

1. **Our theology commends it and our Mission is enhanced by it …**
    There are sound theological and practical reasons for promoting contact and the exchange of ideas, information and resources (including people) between different parts of the Christian family.

---

68 Church of England Guidelines for Companion Links, 2001.

2. **The Church is a family created by God for his purpose**
   Christians have not always been good at such 'receiving', but the church is far more than a collection of individuals. In his vivid image of the *ekklesia* as the body of Christ, St Paul reminded the believers in Rome and Corinth just how much they needed each other. They were not self-sufficient and were not meant to be so. 'The eye cannot say to the hand, I do not need you.'[69]

3. **The Church exists for and by mission**
   The New Testament church knew that it had been created for mission.

4. **We need insights from other cultures**
   In exchanges with companions overseas, some people have already discovered that God can, through other people, reveal insights about himself to which they have, hitherto, been blind. And it works both ways: we all need to learn the lessons that God wants to teach us through others.

5. **We need to encourage one another**
   Hearing what is happening in other places can bring hope, encouragement, enthusiasm, and a vision of new possibilities in a situation where people have ceased to expect change and growth.

6. **We are accountable to one another**
   Normally it is only someone coming from outside who asks the questions about what 'everyone knows to be true', and so enables us to 'stand outside the problem', see ourselves more clearly and question the underlying values and assumptions of our society.

3.29   A large measure of humility is required if we are to take this seriously. Openness to others demands trust, honesty and care, for sometimes hard things may have to be said. If companionship is to work, we have to grant other members of the Body of Christ permission to challenge us in love. What is our responsibility, for example, when the *ekklesia* in any place is overly timid in certain things: evangelism, prophecy, protecting the weak or sharing its resources?

3.30   The Guidelines summarize these points as follows:

- They help break down our insularity and parochialism, our obsession with ourselves and our own concerns.

- They help us take a fresh look at the way we've always done things.

- They help us to see that the Holy Spirit is working in new and different ways all around the world.

- They challenge us to take a fresh look at our own priorities.

- They put a human face on the world-wide church.

- They remind us that we need to receive as well as to give!'[70]

Reviewing these reasons for having Companion Links it is clear that all of them remain valid and pertinent offering sound theological as well as practical reasoning. As they have evolved the central purpose of Companion Links has emerged as primarily friendship expressed through

---

69 Romans 12.3–8; 1 Corinthians 12.
70 *Living Links*, Guidelines for Companion Links, 2001.

visits and exchanges, schools, youth and parish links. As expressed above, one of the major questions about the purpose of Companion Links involves the place of money. It can be argued that money should be part of the Companion Link relationships because it is inconceivable that a friend with more financial resources should not share with one who has less. It can also be argued that money should not form part of a Companion Link relationship because it distorts what is essentially a relationship of friendship. (Chapter 6, entitled 'Receiving and giving', outlines these issues more fully.)

There is a need for greater sharing of good practice concerning the place of money in building Companion Links and involving the Mission Agencies.

What makes for an effective Companion Link?

3.31   The components of effective partnership are as follows:

- **Clear purpose for the partnership agreed and understood by all partners**
  It has been found to be important for all partners in a Link to be clear about the purpose of the Link in order to minimize misunderstanding.

- **Episcopal support and leadership**
  The support of Diocesan Bishops is essential to the establishment and continuation of Companion Links. Bishops provide leadership by example in encouraging parishes to be involved in Diocesan Links, whether Links are with other dioceses in the Anglican Communion or Ecumenical Links. Often Links originate in relationships established between Bishops at the Lambeth Conference. It is then possible for the Link to become embedded in the life of the diocese.

- **Appropriate resourcing at diocesan level**
  Companion Links require planning and co-ordination as well as the execution of complex tasks regarding finance and visa applications for example. Therefore it is not realistic to say that Companion Links do not require staffing (voluntary or paid) or the allocation of financial resources at diocesan level. While Bishops provide leadership for the Link other staff whether voluntary or paid are required to maintain day-to-day administration of the Link as well as envisioning parishes, schools and other groups. If school Links are to be a part of the Link, then good co-operation between Departments of Education and World Mission are essential.

- **Focus, determination and persistence for the long term**
  As with any relationship Companion Links require commitment and determination in order to become effective. Relationships are not achieved without investment of time, resources and effort on all sides. There needs to be a willingness to stay together and work together through difference and tensions. The Swahili word 'Umoja', meaning oneness or unity, describes the togetherness to be worked towards.

- **Willingness to learn from others**
  Companion Links need to be able to learn from others like the Mission Agencies where long-term experience and expertise is held as well as other Companion Links.

  There is also a need to learn across cultures and for parishes in the Church of England to become cross-cultural translators. Chapter 7, entitled 'Becoming Cross-Cultural Christians', suggests ways in which this can be done.

Relationship of Companion Links to Partnership for World Mission

3.32   While it is easy to identify the Mission Agencies as full or associate members of Partnership for World Mission (PWM) it is less easy to identify the Companion Links and few are in contact with PWM regularly apart from the annual conference. When Officers change few dioceses inform PWM and a small number consult PWM when undertaking reviews of Links. It has proved to be difficult to compile a current list of Companion Links with several dioceses with active Links failing to reply to requests for information. This raises issues about the visibility of PWM in the dioceses and strategic questions about how PWM can give added value to Diocesan Companion Links.

The key question for the Diocesan Companion Links concerns how they relate to and learn from each other and the Mission Agencies in the service of the Body of Christ in the global church.

If they are unable to give gifts of money what gifts would they be offering to their partner dioceses?

Relationships between the Mission Agencies and the Companion Links

3.33   Relationships between the Mission Agencies and the Companion Links have been both constructive and challenging. The Agency and the Link approach represent different ways of engaging in world mission relationships. The great value of the approach of the Mission Agencies is the experience they bring from long histories, deep learning, wide understanding and breadth of vision and experience. For example, they will carry experience of the variety of global cultures, and as such can provide resources for training in cross-cultural encounter and in relating across world regions.

3.34   Companion Links with their focus in particular dioceses provide a direct relationship with a particular country or diocese. Companion Links that have existed for some decades build up considerable local expertise which can be offered to others and in practice often are. It is clear that these differing yet complementary approaches can work together and need each other. The regional distribution of Companion Links in Africa shows that the majority of the Links exist in regions where the two generalist Mission Agencies (CMS and USPG) have a history of building the church. Further research is needed to establish what relationship, if any, there is between the presence of the Mission Agencies over many years which has laid the ground for the development of the Companion Links. An interdependent relationship exists between the Mission Agencies and the Companion Links which can be highly creative but also can give rise to tensions. The closer the relationship the more difficult and sustained the tensions can be. There is increasing evidence of effective and increasing working together between the Agencies and Links.

3.35   Where the work of the Companion Links has direct impact on the work of the Mission Agencies several have found the growth of the Companion Links presenting particular challenges. As part of the greater diversification of world mission relationships, perceptions exist that funding that would have gone to the Mission Agencies from parish churches has, instead, gone to the Diocesan Companion Link. It has been argued that Companion Links are part of the donor culture that discourages a breadth of mission engagement.

3.36   One of the General Secretaries of the Mission Agencies has identified certain key questions that require focused discussion in the relationships between Mission Agencies and Companion Links. Though from one Agency these questions have been endorsed by other Mission Agency General Secretaries involved in world mission. They are:

1.   Should the Companion Links become the major funding stream from the Church of England to partners in the world church?

2.   Companion Links by their nature focus their support in particular places to the exclusion of others. What happens to the places that do not have Links and would welcome a Link with a Church of England diocese or parish?

3.   How can Agencies give support to places not covered by Companion Links if funding is not directed towards them?

4.   Do some Links function as Mission Agencies?

5.   What is the added value of the Mission Agencies?

These questions are the subject of ongoing discussion between the Mission Agencies and the Companion Links and need to be discussed in the wider church.

3.37   One of the key differences between Mission Agencies and Companion Links is their respective places in relationship to the diocesan structure of the Church of England and therefore the Diocesan Bishop. While the Voluntary Principle has been a great strength and given great freedom to the Mission Agencies it has also proved to be a constraint because it necessarily distances the Agencies structurally from the ecclesial heart of the Church of England – the Bishop in Synod. Whereas the Companion Link is at the heart of that relationship and the Bishop is often the driver in establishing and developing Companion Links. This is a part of the ministry of a Bishop which

> 'holds in unity the local church with every other local church with which it is in communion'.[71]

In some understandings of church, however, the Bishop in Synod is not the primary location of the local church but it is the local gathered community which comes together under word and sacrament. With this understanding, relationships between the local church in England and overseas are more likely to develop independently of the diocese and its Links.

3.38   The decline in Mission Agency representation at Regional level has reduced the presence of Mission Agencies in the dioceses and, some say, this has contributed to the difficulties in relationships between them. Furthermore this is a picture of ever-increasing diversification, and the emergence of smaller Mission Agencies, with particular focus and minimal staff and overheads and the growing number of parish to parish links, means that there need to be more approaches to world mission relationships represented in discussions about the future.

---

71 *Bishops in Communion: Collegiality in the Service of* Koinonia *in the Church*, House of Bishops' Occasional Paper, Church House Publishing, 2000, p. 12.

How could Mission Agencies and Companion Links work together more effectively?

3.39   To view this question positively it could be asked, What would a good relationship between Companion Links and Mission Agencies look like? A number of marks or features could emerge that would include:

- Where a Mission Agency and a Companion Link share a long-standing commitment to a region, country or diocese of the Anglican Communion there would be sharing of expertise, updating after visits and a development of relationships in the Church of England that assist relationships with a diocese in another part of the Anglican Communion. Where there is a new or emerging Link, the expertise of the Mission Agency can be and often is used in developing cultural understandings and other training. There would be good communication on financial matters. To minimize work in a diocese, funds could be transferred through a Mission Agency which has many years of expertise in this area and has the necessary structures in place to assist in this way. Dioceses could assist in fundraising for Mission Agencies, through Lent Appeals for example, recognizing that the Agencies express Anglican mission identity in a particular way that other bodies do not.

- There would be joint sending and receiving of personnel whether long- or short-term mission partners. Both the Companion Link and the Mission Agency could work together in discernment of vocation and selection, training and preparation of mission partners, sending and support while the mission partner is abroad and re-orientation on return. This could be true of individuals and groups. The Mission Agencies hold great expertise in these areas and particularly in training for mission in Britain and abroad.

- The Companion Links by their nature are focused and particular. It is not possible for the Links to cover all dioceses in the Anglican Communion so it is important to recognize that while the Links provide a particular focus, the Mission Agencies provide a breadth of relationship to areas not covered by Links. This is an important acknowledgement of the strengths and weaknesses of both approaches to world mission relationships.

One of the key issues in relationships between Companion Links and Mission Agencies is how to build mutuality and partnership and to explore the practical ways in which this can be fulfilled.

Living in a crowded landscape

3.40   The world mission relationships of the Church of England form a crowded landscape. Growth is to be welcomed as the Church of England shows itself to be more and more a part of the world church and contributes to the world church with generosity and energy. This increasingly diverse picture arises from a deep desire to serve God and neighbour across cultural boundaries. However, with growth can come tension particularly with regard to funding streams as financial pressures on parishes and individuals become more acute. One of the identifiable tensions in world mission relationships is between the formal channels of engagement such as the Mission Agencies and the Companion Links and the informal, smaller Agencies which stand outside the main channels related to the Church of England and the funding of the formal channels. One of the tensions is the need to identify the appropriate representation through PWM.

3.41   Are these tensions that need to be managed or conflicts that need to be reconciled? Tensions need to be managed in order that they do not develop into conflicts that need to be reconciled. The key is having a tool that can assist in the management of such tensions. CMS has recently been using the tool known as Appreciative Inquiry as a tool to negotiate change and development. The following are questions based on appreciative inquiry that may offer the basis of a tool for negotiating change.

3.42   How could this crowded landscape become less crowded? Effective and intensified communication that builds understanding of different approaches to world mission is vital if the landscape is not to become overcrowded. The annual Partnership for World Mission Conference is an important tool in building such understanding, as are other opportunities for meeting in regions and dioceses. The Mission Agencies have merged or considered merger with others and structural reorganization may become a greater feature of the landscape.

Core questions

- How do we envisage the effective participation of the Church of England in world mission in the future?

- What gives life to world mission engagement at its best?

- What do each of the Agencies and Links contribute to the whole? What are the good news stories?

- Where is there synergy between the different approaches?

- How might that synergy change our current attitudes and practices?

Affirmations

As the Mission Agencies and Diocesan Companion Links of the Church of England we affirm:

- The contribution of each other to God's mission in the world and in particular its expression through the Anglican Communion.

- Our continuing need to listen to and learn from each other in a sustained process of engagement.

Commitments

As the Mission Agencies and Diocesan Companion Links of the Church of England we are committed to:

- Principles of partnership and participation between ourselves based on mutual trust and co-operation for the furthering of God's mission in the world and in particular its expression through the Anglican Communion.

- A continuation of the journey away from former patterns of dependency and towards greater mutuality between ourselves and our partners in the global church.

- Listening to and learning from each other in England and from our global partners.

- The distinctive approach of Anglicanism to world mission based on the sacraments, Scripture and episcopal leadership.

As the Mission Agencies of the Church of England we make commitment to:

- Our continuing journey together in mission asking: What does it mean to live in Covenant today?

- Our continuing life as part of the Church of England and the Anglican Communion.

Recommendations

- That the dioceses of the Church of England and the Mission Agencies work together in partnership including the possibility of raising funds for one or more of the Mission Agencies.

- That the Church of England through the General Synod be reminded of the principle of the Second 5%. That is, if the first 5% of giving is to the parish and diocese, the Second 5% should be directed to the Mission Agencies.

- That attempts are made to draw Anglican Agencies and parishes which are not part of the formal ways of engagement in world mission into the ongoing discussion on paths to mutuality and to use the annual World Mission Conference for this purpose.

Part 2 – Developing New Mission Practices

Chapter 4

Mission and Development

Summary

This chapter offers a holistic theological vision for understanding mission and development using the Five Marks of Mission and Integral Mission. It describes the involvement of the Church of England in development and the importance of language in understanding the differences between mission and development. The chapter concludes by suggesting ways of deepening the dialogue between mission and development.

Understanding mission and development holistically

4.1   'The division between mission and development is a western division that we do not know in Africa. In Africa we do know about the need for flourishing communities that sustain life and we do know about creation which is our life. When creation flourishes we all flourish and when it does not we die. Wholeness and shalom are the ways we talk about life.' Zambian priest

4.2   How can Christian mission and development be understood as complementary approaches to the task of upholding human dignity in the world today? As the quotation above highlights, this is essentially a division that has arisen in Western political and social structures including the churches. Among the Churches in the West it is essential to address this through the building of a theological vision that encompasses different approaches but also acknowledges that difference can be creative. This is a process of building common understanding and identifying ways of working together where that may be fruitful.

4.3   What is the theological vision or imagination that could provide a shared understanding of the resonance between mission and development for the Church of England? The following lenses are offered as the ingredients of a common vision. The thread that runs throughout is the vision for human dignity and flourishing in human society that exists interdependently within God's renewed creation.

Five Marks of Mission

4.4   The Five Marks of Mission provide a broad framework for describing the characteristics of God's mission in the world.

The Five Marks are to

- proclaim the Good News of the Kingdom

- teach, baptize and nurture new believers

- respond to human need by loving service

- seek to transform unjust structures of society

- strive to safeguard the integrity of creation and sustain and renew the life of the earth.

4.5   Each of the Five Marks forms an essential part of the whole mosaic of God's mission that has a clear place for approaches to development in the Christian community. For example, different understandings of mission, such as the work of A Rocha,[72] can encompass proclamation of the Good News of the Kingdom and safeguarding the integrity of creation. These different approaches are held within the overall vision of the *missio dei* or God's mission in the world.

4.6   The specific Marks relating to development concern responding to human need by loving service (Mark 3) and transforming unjust structures of society (Mark 4) as well as safeguarding the integrity of creation and sustaining and renewing the life of the earth (Mark 5). The understanding of mission and development as a dynamic continuum offers the possibility of working with different approaches but also holding together the whole. The various Mission Agencies will have different understandings of mission but will be characterized by a central and explicit understanding of the place of Jesus Christ in their motivation and message as well as a particular relationship to local churches. The Development Agencies that have their origins in Christian faith may choose to use the language of development rather than mission in order to focus their work in areas such as ending poverty. For example, Christian Aid's primary focus is the eradication of poverty and the restoration of justice in the world, which is understood as putting faith into action. There are some fundamental differences concerning the place of faith and particularly Christian faith in human community in these different approaches. However, such differences, clearly understood by all, need not prohibit shared working and understanding. Rather, like the pieces of a mosaic, each piece contributes to the whole image.

Integral Mission

4.7   The lens entitled Integral Mission offers complementary possibilities. In addressing the historical polarities of mission history, Integral Mission advocates that proclamation and social involvement are necessary parts of God's mission in the world and cannot be separated. Integral Mission embodies both evangelism and social involvement.

> 'In integral mission our proclamation has social consequences as we call people to love and repentance in all areas of life. And our social involvement has evangelistic consequences as we bear witness to the transforming grace of Jesus Christ.'[73]

This has given a context within which a Christian Development Agency such as Tearfund has developed a language for the unity of mission and development and explicitness about working with and partnering local churches in countries where they are present. Integral Mission presents the reconciliation of the tension experienced in evangelical understandings of mission between evangelism and social action. However, it may also offer a unifying understanding between mission and development more widely.

---

72 www.arocha.org.
73 The Micah Declaration on Integral Mission and quoted in *The Cape Town Commitment: A Confession of Faith and a Call to Action*, issued by the Third Lausanne Congress on World Evangelization, 16–25 October 2010.

4.8   The differences between development and Christian mission are narrow for some Christian Agencies and wider for others. As such, a holistic understanding can offer a framework for holding together differing emphases while acknowledging and appreciating difference in approach. The understanding of mission as reconciliation also offers an important lens for understanding mission and development as a whole which is at the heart of the Five Marks of Mission and Integral Mission.

4.9   The lenses of both the Five Marks of Mission and Integral Mission offer a possibility for further exploration of the approaches and dynamics of development and mission in the Church of England. While acknowledging differences in approach between Mission and Development Agencies, all are seeking to participate in God's mission in the world. What is envisioned is a situation where there is a climate of continual learning from one another where the best practices of development inform mission and the best practices of mission inform development.

Vision of a just world – the flourishing of creation and human dignity

4.10   The vision of a just world where human persons live interdependently in creation and where each person has the freedom to exercise choice over their lives and faith is a major driver in understandings of mission and development. This vision is expressed variously through the compelling images offered in Scripture as well as through the language of human rights. Scripturally, this vision of a flourishing world where human persons can live with dignity originates, for example, in Isaiah 65.17–25.

Isaiah 65.17–25

New International Version (NIV)

New Heavens and a New Earth

[17] 'See, I will create
new heavens and a new earth.
The former things will not be remembered,
nor will they come to mind.
[18] But be glad and rejoice forever
in what I will create,
for I will create Jerusalem to be a delight
and its people a joy.
[19] I will rejoice over Jerusalem
and take delight in my people;
the sound of weeping and of crying
will be heard in it no more.

[20] 'Never again will there be in it
an infant who lives but a few days,
or an old man who does not live out his years;
the one who dies at a hundred
will be thought a mere child;

the one who fails to reach a hundred
will be considered accursed.
²¹ They will build houses and dwell in them;
they will plant vineyards and eat their fruit.
²² No longer will they build houses and others live in them,
or plant and others eat.
For as the days of a tree,
so will be the days of my people;
my chosen ones will long enjoy
the work of their hands.
²³ They will not labour in vain,
nor will they bear children doomed to misfortune;
for they will be a people blessed by the LORD,
they and their descendants with them.
²⁴ Before they call I will answer;
while they are still speaking I will hear.
²⁵ The wolf and the lamb will feed together,
and the lion will eat straw like the ox,
and dust will be the serpent's food.
They will neither harm nor destroy
on all my holy mountain,
says the Lord.'

4.11   This is a vision of human living that is centred on peace (v 25 using animal imagery to depict the absence of conflict), health (v 21 where child mortality and premature death will be a thing of the past), work (vv 21–22 where the fruit of labour will be just and the harvest will be fruitful) and the absence of exploitation (v 22). These are the prerequisites for human dignity and flourishing set out in the prophecy of Isaiah that have considerable resonance for today. The vision for the end to poverty is another way of expressing a vision for human flourishing based on peace, health, work and the absence of exploitation. In other words, a vision of human dignity rooted in all peoples being made in the image of God where inequality and lack of the basic needs of human living are a scandal. Likewise, the vision for the flourishing of people in community sharing faith in Jesus Christ has led the Mission Agencies to focus on peace, health, work and the absence of exploitation as a way of expressing their vision of human flourishing in community. Another way of seeing that same question is considering the nature of our vision of redeemed humanity. Christian anthropology is concerned with visions for human flourishing and dignity and understandings of both mission and development carry such vision. For this to be realized, the backdrop is an interdependent relationship of redeemed humanity living within a flourishing creation. The eschatological vision underlying this is, 'With all wisdom and understanding, he made known to us the mystery of his will according to his good pleasure, which he purposed in Christ, to be put into effect when the times reach their fulfilment – to bring unity to all things in heaven and on earth under Christ' (Ephesians 1.9–11 NIV).

4.12   The Great Commandment (Matthew 22.37–40)[74] sets out the relational pattern for human flourishing. These three commands are best understood interdependently with 'Love the Lord your God' forming the basis for the love of neighbour and self. They are all part of the one Commandment and the linking of neighbour and self also highlights the relationship between the powerful and the powerless. One person's denial of dignity through structural power differentials

---

74 Deuteronomy 6.5; Mark 12.30; Luke 10.27.

is also the denial of the dignity of the other. As the Archbishop of Canterbury has stressed, linking human dignity to the image of the Body in St Paul,

> 'the welfare of each individual and the welfare of all are inseparable, so that the poverty of another is also *my* diminution and the liberation of the other is likewise mine as well'.[75]

Both mission and development seek to address the effects of the fallout from broken relationship and the search for reconciliation with God, with creation and with humanity.

Fullness of life

4.13   Christ's gift of fullness or abundance (John 10.10) offers a specifically Christological promise of life within human community. The context for Christ's declaration about the purpose of his coming to bring fullness of life is the parable about him as the gate to the sheepfold. One Congolese commentator states that this is a picture which gives an image of human community under Christ.

> 'Victory over poverty, denial of identity, exclusion, fragility, the final disappearance of all these troubles, are not synonymous with "life in abundance"; but it is in face of these realities and despite them, opposing them and going beyond them that Johannine theology articulates the quality of trust in God – a God who lends our finite lives a fullness of meaning and truth that no extravagance of bread, no orgy by the powers-that-be can give them.'[76]

4.14   This is a key verse for the understanding of mission and development as a unity in the life of the church. It means that in Christ is found the fullest dignity open to humankind. In the person of Christ fullness and self-emptying (*kenosis*) are part of the same dynamic of service. Though the kenosis of Christ has particular meaning relating to his divinity there is a relevance to human experience where to empty oneself is to receive Christ's fullness. Both mission and development are concerned with the good news of the possibility of fullness of life for all people. In our current institutional and Agency structures these emphases are expressed differently while not denying the whole message that Christ brings. Mission and Development Agencies seek to challenge and change the life-denying forces that diminish human community including ecological destruction.

4.15   Arguably one of the most pressing issues between mission and development concerns the nature and practice of some forms of Christian evangelism. Many would maintain an important distinction between evangelism and proselytism.[77] Examples include the donation of aid which is conditional upon conversion to Christian faith or aid being given exclusively to Christians. The recently published document *Christian Witness in a Multi-Religious World: Recommendations for Conduct* presents an ethical framework for Christian evangelism that

---

75 'New Perspectives on Faith and Development', a speech given to the Tony Blair Foundation, 12 November 2009.

76 Kabongo-Mbaya, Study Text for the World Alliance of Reformed Churches Accra Convention, 2004, www.warc/accra2004.

77 Proselytism is understood here as the act of attempting to convert another with pressure or the presence of incentives. For a fuller discussion of the nature of proselytism see the World Council of Churches document 'The Challenge of Proselytism' found at *www.oikoumene.org/en/.../challenge-of-proselytism.html.*

makes this distinction clearly. The Mission and Development Agencies may consider a joint study of the document *Christian Witness in a Multi-religious World Recommendations for Conduct*.[78]

Diakonia

4.16   Understanding mission and development as service is to come to the heart of human dignity. For one person to serve another is to impart value and dignity in actions of giving and receiving that have life-giving implications for individuals and communities. Three questions from Luke's Gospel can guide thinking in this area. In the parable of the Good Samaritan (Luke 10.25–37) the question is: Who is my neighbour? The reply that Jesus gives reveals the breadth of the nature of neighbour love. It goes far beyond the perceived boundaries that human community constructs to include those excluded and rejected.

4.17   The second question is: Who is the greatest? (Luke 22.24–27). Again Jesus turns common assumptions upside down making service the essence of his ministry. In following the call and pattern of Christ all mission and ministry is about self-giving service in the world. Development and mission are characterized by sacrificial service and giving that has the potential to overturn the deleterious patterns and structures of the world.

4.18   The third question concerns the healing of the ten lepers (Luke 17.11–19). Jesus' question, 'Where are the other nine?' concerns those who failed to thank Jesus after their healing. Here is an example of thankfulness opening up a place of encounter with Christ. It is the Samaritan who comes back to Jesus to give thanks and praise. The other nine were healed but experienced only half of the story. Service and thankfulness are intimately linked and open the possibility of deeper encounter. Transformation is the fruit of thanksgiving for what we have and engenders hope in the face of deeply intractable situations. Thanksgiving is often witnessed among those who have few material resources but who have an abundance of hope in God. With these three questions Jesus indicates the scope, context and manner of service in human community.

4.19   The idea of prophetic *diakonia* goes beyond the common perception of Christian service as serving individuals but not necessarily including a global perspective. It gathers together the global and local implications that sees acts of service as building justice.

> '*Diakonia* is central to what it means to be the church ... while diakonia begins as unconditional service to the neighbour in need, it leads inevitably to social change that restores, reforms and transforms ... a theology of the cross calls things what they really are, moving beyond politeness and pretence, breaking the silence and taking the risk of speaking truth to power, even when this threatens the established order and results in hardship or persecution.'[79]

Prophetic *diakonia* is closely related to proclamation and partnership. Partnership engenders the strength of voice with which to confront the world powers where proclamation of the good news and the call to justice go hand in hand.

---

78 Published by the World Council of Churches, Pontifical Council for Interreligious Dialogue and the World Evangelical Alliance, 28 June 2011, www.oikoumene.org.
79 Lutheran World Federation Johannesburg Consultation on Prophetic Diakonia, *For the Healing of the Nations*, 2002, p. 6.

Mission, Development and the Church of England

4.20   The Mission Agencies of the Church of England and the Ecumenical Development Agencies have brought many opportunities to the Churches in Britain and Ireland that have enriched their common life as well as making a difference in the wider world. The associations and alliances that have created movements such as Jubilee 2000 and Make Poverty History have given many Christians the opportunity to express their discipleship in the context of working for a just world and confronting unjust structures. As well as these recent high-profile events, there has been the continuing work of the Mission Agencies for some hundreds of years in working with churches and local communities in many parts of the world. More recently, the emergence of Development Agencies such as Christian Aid and Tearfund has made a considerable difference to communities throughout the world.

4.21   Previous chapters have outlined the changes and developments in mission theology and practice. Development practice is similarly a fast-changing area. Since 2000 the Millennium Development Goals (MDGs) have provided a framework and a measurable point of reference for development work. The eight MDGs form a blueprint agreed to by all the world's countries and leading development institutions. They range from halving extreme poverty to halting the spread of HIV/AIDS and providing universal primary education – all by the target date of 2015. With such global momentum, the MDGs have provided a framework for many churches in the Anglican Communion to help provide practical shape to their missional response to global poverty. Some of the MDGs have seen significant progress; others, especially in relation to maternal and child health, are seriously lagging.

Development in the structures of the Church of England

4.22   The Church of England has a long history, at all levels, with involvement in both mission and development issues. At parish level the clearest expression of involvement in development has been through the annual Christian Aid week door-to-door collection where parishes throughout England provide volunteers to collect funds from those who would not necessarily have allegiance to the Christian faith. This is viewed by many parishes as an important part of their mission and is carried out sacrificially year by year. For many at parish level the terms mission and development would be understood interchangeably as two sides of the same coin. In some parish churches the natural allegiance would be to Agencies such as Tearfund[80] as a Christian Development Agency with an evangelical understanding of development and mission as holistic or integral mission. A vital part of the expression of mission and development at local level are the relationships created as a result of working together and breaking down barriers.

4.23   At diocesan level engagement with mission and development at parish level is supported in some dioceses through an adviser in world development. In an increasingly difficult financial climate with merger of posts such a post holder may also have responsibilities in world mission and the Diocesan Companion Link. The level of diocesan support varies considerably and with ever-increasing pressure on resources these posts are likely to be taken by clergy in addition to parish responsibilities or by lay volunteers. A national network of Development Advisers works to provide national co-ordination of diocesan activities and an important channel of communication

---

80 Tearfund became an Associate Member of Partnership for World Mission in 2011.

between national and diocesan levels. A very valuable resource is the biannual world development conference that is organized ecumenically by a team from Development Agencies and dioceses among others. This national network is closely linked to the mission networks. It is proposed that Partnership for World Mission be open to Agencies involved in development as well as mission. Despite commitment to the task of mission, tensions exist at diocesan level about the differing approaches to mission and development. Many of the Diocesan Companion Links are involved in funding and assisting projects in their Link Dioceses which could be understood as development. It is at diocesan level that the differences between national institutions become both less and more important. They become less important because the focus turns to practical local delivery in parishes and more important because different messages from Agencies at national level can make that vital local delivery more complex.

4.24   In 2004 the Archbishop of Canterbury established a Secretariat for International Development at Lambeth Palace to serve and extend his ministry in relation to issues of global poverty, justice and peace building as an integral part of the church's mission in the world. This office helps to resource the Archbishop's policy and advocacy work, focusing particularly on support to the church's response in conflict-affected states. It works in close collaboration with the Anglican Communion Office and the Mission and Public Affairs Division International Affairs desk. The 2008 Lambeth Conference called for the establishment of an instrument for co-ordination of relief and development work in the Anglican Communion. The Anglican Alliance for Development, Relief and Advocacy was launched in January 2011, its development co-ordinated by the Archbishop's International Development Secretariat, the Anglican Communion Office and the MPA International Affairs desk, with a Steering Group drawn from churches and Mission and Development Agencies around the Communion. The Church of England Mission Agencies are involved in the continuing development and governance of the Alliance. Throughout its inception, it has been stressed that the Anglican Alliance is concerned with adding value by providing a space for exchange of experience and wisdom, whereby the capacity of local churches in the global North and South to respond to poverty and injustice can be advanced. It is not an independent Agency or fund-giving body, but rather a forum 'bringing together the Anglican family of churches and Agencies to work for a world free of poverty and injustice'. Through a series of consultations in the global regions the Alliance is already making a significant difference to relationships in the Anglican Communion. The emphasis in the global consultations has been on the global regions themselves setting their own priorities in relief and development.

4.25   At national level the Church of England has expressed its commitment to development ecumenically through Christian Aid. Acting in development on behalf of the churches, Christian Aid has developed into a major Development Agency since its formation by the British and Irish churches in 1948. At certain points questions have been raised by the Churches of Britain and Ireland and the Church of England Mission Agencies about the relationship of Christian Aid to its roots in the churches and Christian faith. Recent developments at Christian Aid have seen a greater openness to hearing and responding to such concerns and a willingness to engage with them further. In 2011 Christian Aid held a significant Consultation specifically addressing its partnerships with Anglican Churches in the African context. Specific recommendations have been made which envisage a greater dialogue between Christian Aid and its Anglican partners.[81] Christian Aid has also been working to develop its theological base and build a deeper understanding of what partnership is in its context. A deeper level of dialogue between Christian Aid, the Mission Agencies, the Church of England and the wider ecumenical bodies continues to develop.

---

81 *Christian Aid – Anglican Partnerships Consultation*, 15–17 Nairobi March 2011.

Areas for further exploration

4.26   A number of key questions have been raised concerning the relationships between the Anglican Mission Agencies and the Christian-inspired Development Agencies. These questions need focused attention in order to develop creative future joint working and to provide clarity and transparency at diocesan and parish level. This creative future-oriented energy will be concerned with learning from one another and doing theology together as well as sharing good practice. It will also concern learning from the churches at local level.

The specific areas are:

- What opportunities are available for mutual learning between the Mission Agencies and the Christian-inspired Development Agencies recognizing their different yet mutual and complementary areas of work as part of God's mission in the world?

- What issues provide opportunities for building coalitions and partnerships?

- How can the Anglican Mission Agencies and Christian-inspired Development Agencies work together to enable effective delivery of projects and campaigns at local church level in England and internationally?

- These questions, and others, could become the basis of discussion between the Anglican Mission Agencies, Diocesan Companion Links and the Christian based Development Agencies in a Mission and Development Discussion Forum under the umbrella of Partnership for World Mission.

Mission and Development – affirmations and commitments

Affirmations

The members of PWM, comprising the Anglican Mission Agencies and Diocesan Companion Links affirm:

- The Five Marks of Mission as a means of embracing the complementary yet distinctive approaches to God's mission in the world.

- The establishment of the Anglican Alliance for Relief and Development as a means of co-operation and shared learning within the Anglican Communion as an expression of our participation in God's mission.

- The engagement of the Church of England in the ongoing ecumenical work of Christian Aid and other Agencies to tackle poverty and to embrace life in all its fullness.

Commitments

The members of PWM, comprising the Anglican Mission Agencies and Diocesan Companion Links commit to:

- Continuing dialogue and action between the Mission Agencies, Companion Links and the Christian-inspired Development Agencies on the role of the local church around the world in their respective work areas.

- Working through the Anglican Alliance for Relief, Development and Advocacy to assist partnership in areas of particular need.

- Developing understandings of mutuality in mission and development and recognizing the gifts received as well as those given.

Conclusion

Current discussions between some of the Anglican Mission Agencies and Christian Aid signal a positive note for the building of mutual understanding and joint working in the future. Built on the foundations of mutually appreciated theological vision, different approaches can be a creative spur in future dialogue. The ultimate purpose of such dialogue is the building of a just world and participation in God's work of reconciliation in the world.

Chapter 5

Hearing from Our Partners

Summary

This chapter introduces some of the voices of the churches in the Majority World to the discussion of the future of world mission relationships in the Church of England. It considers what the Church of England can learn from her Majority World partners. In conclusion, different ways of understanding world mission are suggested which include friendship.

5.1   Mission is not a one-way street. It involves relationships – many relationships – with God and people and a multitude of different contexts. Relationships in mission involve crossing boundaries with all the inherent complexities. Such relationships are at the heart of Christian mission. They are concerned with the local – the situations and contexts where people live their daily lives and interact with others. Mission is not an ethereal, abstract process but rather is local, embedded in real life and is shaped by the forces, dilemmas and histories that affect different contexts. Understanding local contexts is crucial to this process. Listening to the voice of the other, who, in Christ may become our friend, is at the heart of world mission relationships. Those coming to particular situations from the outside can often see issues and circumstances confronting particular communities in new ways that can open new perspectives and possibilities.

5.2   This chapter reflects and builds on the theological understandings of Chapters 1 and 2. These are that Christian mission is rooted in God's nature and being as Trinity. Mission is God's first and foremost and is expressed in a diverse set of relationships and activities. God's church in response to the generous and loving mission of God is called to participate in God's mission in the world. Hospitality and proclamation are the modes or praxis through which such mission is enacted expressing the partnership between God and the church and between churches globally. Understanding mission as reconciliation is another way of understanding these movements of transformation towards wholeness.

5.3   This chapter will feature voices from the Church of England's partners in the Anglican Communion as well as the voices of other churches. It will address the central question of how listening to our partners affects the way the Church of England conducts its world church relationships and how the Church of England is called to deepen and develop its approach and practice in world mission. How can the Church of England deepen our worldwide relationships in the service of God's mission and service to our neighbour? How can our worldwide relationships assist the Church of England in service and mission within English society?

5.4   Relationships across cultures involve facing essential and sometimes uncomfortable questions in order for such relationships to grow in the likeness of Christ. One of the most difficult aspects of cross cultural relationships is language. It is necessary to constantly ask: Are we hearing each other rightly? Language is rooted in particular contexts and cultures and even the use of the same word in the same language can have different meanings in different places. Despite these complexities, engaging in cross-cultural relationships can be a life-changing process but requires persistence and perseverance. Does listening to our partners mean accepting everything they say as right and true? What if we disagree with the partners' analysis of our situation? Listening does not always result in complete agreement and there is no absolute obligation to accept all that is brought or said. However, each has to be authentic in their particular mission situation and speak out of personal and corporate experience. When this happens, dialogue can happen that brings about changed perspectives. In the process of evaluating what another brings, new insights can be achieved and it is this that bears fruit in hearing the voice of the Spirit for today. An example of this process is the publication *Voices from Africa*,[82] which brought together different voices from parts of Africa and reflections from the Church of England. As the Archbishop of York writes in the conclusion,

> 'It is important for us in the West to hear the authentic voices of Africa, without our own priorities and concerns providing the agenda for our interest.'[83]

Seven 'ingredients of true partnership'

5.5 The Partnership for World Mission Conference in 2010 considered 'The Future of Partnership' and the keynote speaker was The Bishop of Harare, the Rt Revd Chad Gandiya. He brought his valuable perspectives on being in a partnership relationship with the Church of England. Bishop Chad placed his comments within current global movements in Christianity,

> 'the issue of partnership has become crucial in the face of the acknowledged new shift in Christianity's centre of gravity to the non-Western world'.[84]

This shift away from the global north and west as the centre of Christianity has highlighted differences between the materially resource-rich global North West where the church on the whole is declining and the Majority World where church growth is consistent and rapid.

Bishop Chad goes on to emphasize seven 'ingredients of true partnership'. He says,

> 'When we put together biblical and modern conceptions of partnership we come up with at least seven ingredients of what constitutes true partnership.
>
> 1. In the Bible partnership is only possible between parties which, while maintaining their individual identities, are nevertheless compatible with one another. In partnership there is no thought of one eclipsing the other's identity and remaking them in their own image. Partnership accepts and celebrates the differences between the parties.
>
> 2. Partnership assumes a task or a mission that can better be accomplished when two or more parties work together than when one party works alone. In 1 Corinthians 8.23 Paul describes Titus as "my partner, who works with me to serve you". It was the viable partnership between Paul and Titus that enabled both Paul and Titus to fully participate in mission. In other words, without a specific and agreed vision or task partnership would not make sense.
>
> 3. Partnership is meant to be mutually beneficial and not a one sided affair. In Philippians 4.14–16 Paul, who had benefitted the Philippians by planting their Church

---

82 Wheeler (ed.), *Voices from Africa*, Church House Publishing, PWM, CMS and USPG, 2002.
83 Wheeler, *Voices from Africa*, p. 137.
84 'The Future of Partnership', delivered 1 November 2010, Partnership for World Mission Conference.

now talks of benefitting from partnership with that same church. A relationship in which one party does all the giving and the other does all the receiving does not qualify to be called a partnership but perhaps a "donor/recipient" relationship. Not so long ago, a certain Christian leader came up to me and said, "You know we can help your diocese a lot. My diocese has a lot of money. Let us establish a partnership between our dioceses. When you get home send me an email with a list of projects you need financial assistance for." I don't doubt that he meant it but for me that was not the kind of relationship or "partnership" I wanted to establish between our dioceses and so I let it pass for a while. We met again a while later and he reiterated his offer and I suggested that his diocese made a donation to my diocese without going into building a partnership relationship as our understanding of partnership was quite different.

4. Partners must stay faithful to one another. True partnership is built on mutual trust and faithful commitment to one another. Unfortunately, a lot of so-called partnerships are built on suspicion and mistrust and as a result they do not last.

5. The fifth biblical requirement for partnership is mutual respect that is built on the foundation of equality between the partners. The English may have invented the game of soccer/football and may be very crazy about the game as you witness every weekend. Partnership in most mission organizations is like this game but played on a mountain slope pitch. The Mission Agencies goal posts they are defending are at the top while those of the so-called partners are at the bottom of the slope. Who is going to win the game and why? There is no equality whatsoever between the two teams. No matter how hard the so called partners try, they will not score against the Mission Agencies. The playing field has to be level. In a partnership none has all the strengths while the other has all the weaknesses.

6. It follows from the above that each partner involves the other in decisions that can affect the partnership so that each can own the outcome. There is a need to go beyond the rhetoric of partners and partnership in mission. Many so-called partners are directly or indirectly involved in raising funds from which they benefit but often are kept in the dark about how much has been raised and are not involved in deciding how those funds should be used. This raises a fundamental question. Whose resources are they in the first place? God's or ours? Can we not both be stewards of the very same resources, i.e. in the distribution by the Church or Mission Agencies and use by the partners or recipients? If we are not careful we may be wittingly or unwittingly encouraging a "baas" (boss) and "boy" relationship that is simply camouflaged by the more respectable term "partnership".

7. The current global financial crisis has put partnership on the spotlight and exposed cracks that were hidden in the relationship. It has exposed some of the flaws in some understandings or misunderstanding of true partnership. For example, when an organization or Mission Agency is in financial crisis, does it discuss the crisis with the so called partners and try and find a solution together or not? The tendency has been to give the impression that they alone know the extent of the crisis and the urgency with which the matter has to be dealt with and then inform 'partners' what needs to be done and they have to appreciate that they have not come to that decision easily. Is that how partners work with each other? Is money the only ingredient to a relationship? Surely, if you are true partners you journey together through thick and thin. Unfortunately, it seems to me that we might have baptized 'donor/recipient' relationship into 'partnership' relationship with no change to the way we operate. A

change in label does not necessarily make a difference to the way people operate. A change of views or attitude is necessary.

In Zimbabwe people talk about both the curse and blessings of having diamonds. The precious stone becomes a blessing when it is used to improve the lives of people and the nation. However, it becomes a curse when people suffer because of the diamonds discovered in your village and surrounding areas. In some cases the affluence of the Western Church can also equally be a curse or a blessing. It can be a curse if it keeps for itself what God so generously has put in its hands and gives away only the crumbs which are falling from its tables. Unfortunately, money has become a very influential factor in doing mission in partnership. The western church or Mission Agencies should not think that mission can be done with western money and third world personnel.'[85]

This extensive quotation brings to the forefront of this argument the importance of interdependence and mutuality in global relationships and how a lack of attentiveness to the differences and subtleties in such relationships can have harmful effects. Yet again the reality of the unintended consequences of certain actions on the part of one or other of the parties is evident.

5.6   These reflections on partnerships between churches in the North-West and South and East are echoed in the ecumenical context of the Edinburgh 2010 World Mission Conference. Fidon Mwombeki, Director of the United Evangelical Mission[86] spoke at the conference about the experience of mission personnel from the South to the North. From the German perspective he spoke of the persistence of ideas of Europe as a Christian continent for whom mission is

'giving money to some mission organization which does it on their behalf'.

Mission for many in the mainline Protestant denominations, he argues, is about giving money to the poor and so those from the South have little to give to the resource-rich European churches.

Speaking of the encounter between missionaries from the South and Europe he describes how difficult it is for those from the South to be received as serious contributors to church life and how it is

'complicated for the North to say explicitly what they need from their Southern colleagues'.

While the material needs of the South are easier to identify (though not always accurately by European visitors), Europeans find it difficult to articulate what they need from those of the global South.

5.7   Though speaking of the German context, many of these comments would be echoed by those from the South who come to the Church of England. A visitor from Latin America to their Companion Diocese in England was heard to express concern that the English congregations did not say what they needed from their Latin American Christian brothers and sisters. It was always the Latin Americans who had to state their needs and receive, which did not result in mutual encounter and exchange.

---

85 From a paper entitled 'The Future of Partnership', delivered at the Partnership for World Mission Conference, 2010.
86 UEM is a joint mission of 33 churches from Asia (15) Africa (12) and Germany (6).

5.8   A voice from India reflected after the Edinburgh 2010 World Mission Conference,

> 'The time has come where we need to listen to people who are receiving mission. Mission should not be from those who are missioning but from the viewpoints of those that are being missioned.'[87]

5.9   Another voice reflecting on the experience of partnership of the Church of South India and the Western churches says that

> 'Four factors need to be present in order to have mature relationships in mission, namely, mutuality, reciprocity, advocacy and solidarity and transparency ... It is the shift from becoming religious colonizers to becoming religious neighbours.'[88]

A message for the Church of England?

5.10   Despite long experience of the use of the language of partnership, older models of thinking and practice in world mission have been remarkably persistent. While many involved in The Church of England's world mission thinking and practice have a high level of awareness of the importance of mutuality in mission and have taken steps to move forward from donor–recipient models it has proved difficult to change well-established thinking particularly at parish level. Two pieces of research shed light on this situation. The first is *Foundations for Mission* which involved the conducting of one-to-one interviews with sixteen local church leaders from eight denominations. It became apparent from this data that while the church leaders interviewed showed an awareness of some of the complexities of relationships across cultures they recorded that many in their congregations understood mission as the developed West doing good for poor people in other parts of the world. There was little indication that mission could be understood and practised as a reciprocal relationship characterized by mutual giving and receiving.

5.11   The second research project, entitled *Finding Frames: New ways to engage the UK public in global poverty*, concludes that from successive surveys of the UK public it has become clear that

> 'The causes of poverty are seen as internal to poor countries: famine, war, natural disasters, bad governance, over-population and so on. The dominant paradigm has been labelled the Live Aid Legacy, characterized by the relationship of "Powerful Giver and Grateful Receiver". Public perceptions have been stuck in this frame for 25 years.'[89]

5.12   This research analyses the linguistic frameworks that surround attitudes to global poverty alleviation in the UK and finds that in the UK population 24% of the population are very concerned about global poverty and 14% are most concerned. It is likely that Christians make up a proportion of those in the very or most concerned categories. However,

> 'Even engaged people can't sustain a conversation about debt, trade or aid for long.'[90]

5.13   What are the frames which dominate the Church of England's thinking about mission as, for example, development, reconciliation or prophetic dialogue? It is reasonable to assume a

---

87 Bharath Patta, *Council for World Mission Journal*, edn 58, July 2010.
88 Revd Dr Leslie Nathaniel, *Magazine of the Friends of the Church in India*, August 2010, no. 37, p. 39.
89 Darnton and Kirk, *Finding Frames*, Chapter 1, p. 6.
90 *Finding Frames*, p. 6.

certain degree of resonance with the conclusions of the Finding Frames research as it is likely that many of those who register a high degree of commitment to development are likely to come from the churches. Therefore, it can reasonably be assumed that these attitudes also persist even among those who have a high level of awareness of global poverty. Anecdotal evidence from many sources also bears this out. There is a need for the Church of England to examine and reflect upon its frames for thinking about mission, including money and the effect that it has upon world mission relationships. To what extent will the dominant patterns of thinking in the world also dominate the thinking of Christians or will images and models of the church as worldwide communion and the Body of Christ inform current thinking and practice. While some of the reservations expressed above about the causes of global poverty may contain an element of truth, even so Christian thinking and practice should view our partners in the worldwide church as our brothers and sisters who exhibit in their life joys and failings just as the Church of England does.

5.14   One of the persistent frames employed in the West concerns negative images of the continents and countries such as Africa, Latin America, the Indian sub-continent and the Far East. A young Kenyan priest writes,

> 'the continent of Africa is often summarized in pictures of gloom. It is the dark, if not dangerous, continent where death and disease are almost taken for granted. It is where corruption is endemic and savage brutality is to be expected. It is a place where almost nothing works where positive news is a miracle. While it is a fact that Africa struggles with crucial issues of poverty, corruption, poor leadership and HIV/Aids it is also true that the continent struggles with the dark and hopeless image that the world knows; the continent struggles to show her countless blessings, riches, diversity, happy moments and unique contribution to the household of God where ideally every member and all faith communities are equal. It is not about right or wrong but the failure to recognize that there are occasions when Africa laughs because of its peoples' own efforts. This image affects the continent's role as a partner and agent of mission.'[91]

5.15   What are the images and perceptions of Africa, for example, that the Church of England projects in the communities in England? All who have experienced the riches of these continents and their churches in England must, as part of God's mission, begin to develop the frames that our communities adopt when speaking of them. Do we hear and listen to the good in other parts of the world? Are we blind to the glaring problems we face at home? This is one way in which we can change the mission imagination.

Experiencing partnership

5.16   For many who have experienced partnerships with dioceses, Agencies and churches it has felt all too often like a perpetuation of colonial models. There has been a lack of transparency and trust which has disabled working as the Body of Christ. Partnership relationships with the Church of England can be summed up as on one hand great generosity and on the other a reserve that is difficult to get beyond.

5.17   The Revd Robert Kereopa, Executive Officer of the Board of Anglican Mission for the Anglican Church in Aotearoa, New Zealand and Polynesia gave the following indicators to the

---

91 Irene Ayallo, in *Life-Widening Mission Global Anglican Perspectives*, ed. Ross, Regnum, 2012.

2011 Partnership for World Mission Conference for the development of the practice of partnership in the Western churches. They are

> 'Practice the seven principles of partnership, up-skill cross-culturally and seek to serve before you seek to control.'[92]

5.18   The Archbishop of Canterbury, addressing the 150th anniversary of the Anglican Church in Japan, spoke of the action of one of the early pioneer Bishops to Japan, Edward Bickersteth, who removed his shoes when doing a private confirmation. The Archbishop remarked,

> 'We could say that in many contexts the Christian mission arrived not only wearing heavy shoes but quite ready to tread on as many feet as possible. Perhaps mission is truly effective only when it comes with bare feet.'

After talking about the need to tread lightly in mission and the importance of simplicity, risk and solidarity he outlined the need for

> 'reverence comes third. We approach our neighbours not with arrogance and impatience but with a readiness to learn and a willingness to rejoice in the rich texture of their human lives, individual and cultural. We look and listen for God in all that lies before us.'

5.19   The first question for all involved in cross-cultural mission is: What type of shoes are we wearing? Though we may think we are wearing slippers, our footprint can so often bear the mark of walking boots to others. As mentioned in earlier chapters it is important to acknowledge the negative footprint as one that is unintended. Unintended consequences are often the result of honourable intentions that take an unanticipated turn.

Walking a different path

5.20   The Church of England is being called now to walk a different path. There is an urgent need to find a third space between the new colonialism, which is understood as the domination of resources, and the cultural hegemony by the North and West and the lives of those in the Majority World living without the power and influence that money brings. An emerging theme in mission theology suggests that the third space is friendship. Professor Dana Robert describes friendship as the

> 'hidden component of twentieth-century missions'.[93]

Furthermore, she writes,

> 'with the end of European colonialism, organizational trends like "partnership" and "partners in mission" replaced friendship as a suitable ethic for a postcolonial age'.

5.21   Perhaps the next phase in world mission relationships for the Church of England is an emphasis on the priority of the values of friendship and hospitality from which comes the mutual receiving and giving of the gifts of the Kingdom. Chapter 2 outlined the shift from partnership to participation and hospitality and stressed that these are all aspects of the churches calling from

---

92 Given at the Partnership for World Mission Conference, 1 November 2011.
93 Dana Robert, 'Cross-Cultural Friendship in the Creation of Twentieth-Century World Christianity', *International Bulletin of Missionary Research*, vol. 35, April 2010, p. 101.

God and the need to reflect such a calling in our relationships. Friendship is one of the practical expressions.

5.22   Such a shift would have particular implications for present practice. In theological reflection what would be the interpretation of Jesus' words regarding friendship in John 15.15 (NIV) in the context of a postcolonial and neocolonial world? 'I no longer call you servants, because a servant does not know his master's business. Instead, I have called you friends, for everything that I learned from my Father I have made known to you.'

5.23   A turn to friendship would mean exploring the nature of our current relationships and asking our partners the question: Are we friends? Or how would we describe our relationships? What types or styles of friendship are being envisaged? What is the nature of institutional friendship and is such possible? What are the possibilities of friendship in world mission when historical relationships have been characterized by asymmetry in the context of colonial rule? A focus on friendship would emphasize relationship over projects and would call all world mission practitioners to ask the question about the impact of funding on cross-cultural friendships as part of project planning. What changes could be brought about by using the word 'friendship' every time we now use the word 'partnership'?

5.24   Friendship is a vital part of the work of the Companion Links and Mission Agencies and other styles of world mission relationships. However, what is being considered here is whether it has untapped possibility as a means of drawing Christ's church into deeper relationship reflecting the nature of the triune God and for the sake of God's mission in the world. As Robert concludes,

> 'In today's world of instant communication, short attention spans, and material development as mission, the sacrificial practices of friendship stand as evidence for the kingdom ethics of God's love for all people.'[94]

Affirmations

The Church of England at national, diocesan, parish, Agency and network level affirms the importance of close and attentive listening in nurturing relationships across cultures as an expression of our communion in the Body of Christ.

Commitments

The Church of England at national, diocesan, parish, Agency and network level commits to the process of listening across cultures using methods such as Indaba to facilitate such listening and learning.

---

94 Robert, 'Cross-Cultural Friendship in the Creation of Twentieth-Century World Christianity', p. 106.

Chapter 6

Receiving and Giving

Summary

This chapter will explore the many forms of giving and receiving that make up an important part of world mission relationships. It will then explore the biblical story of Paul's collection for the church in Jerusalem focusing on 2 Corinthians 8—9 and will ascertain key learning points for the practices of giving and receiving today. The chapter will then address some of the key issues around financial giving. It will argue that cultural differences surrounding finance need a greater understanding in the development of world mission relationships in the Church of England.

Different ways of receiving and giving

6.1   Receiving and giving is all about relationship. What we receive and give are the tangible, practical ways of expressing relationship and the ways in which relationships are nurtured. The many ways in which we receive and give include worship and prayer, meals, skills and money, to name only a few. There is a deep joy to be experienced in receiving and giving which builds relationship in all their many forms including relationships in world mission. For Christians we are primarily receivers of the grace of God through the gift of his Son Jesus Christ. All our giving and receiving has roots in the movement of God's gift and grace. The receiving and giving of money has to be understood in this context.

6.2   With the growth in different forms of world mission relationships between the Church of England and many parts of the Anglican Communion there has also been a growth in the ways and means of giving and receiving. The fundamental model that the Church of England has worked within since the 1950s in its world mission relationships is partnership. Earlier chapters have outlined the background to partnership and its strengths and weaknesses regarding its use in relationships of giving and receiving. Partnership relationships have been conducted through two major means of giving and receiving – people and money. The Anglican Mission Agencies and the Diocesan Companion Links provide the major structures for giving and receiving. Structures are a formalized or institutional way of expressing types or styles of relationship. Within these structures giving and receiving has been expressed historically through the sending of people, largely from the Church of England, through the Anglican Mission Agencies to other parts of the world. Today one of the changing patterns in world mission relationships can be found in sending people as more and more churches in the Majority World are sending mission partners to Europe including England. There are also many people who have come to England from other parts of the world and are involved in migrant and indigenous churches here. The Church of England has received ministers from the Majority World for some time and is developing this practice within the Anglican Communion for ministry in parishes.

6.3   One of the strengths of partnership as a framework is its flexibility. It can be understood as a business or formal relationship or as a friendship. In practice, partnership has worked somewhere between these two ends of the spectrum. Many of those who are sending or giving are those who need to give public account for their activities and therefore giving and receiving has involved formal agreements and understandings. The question has to be asked, however, whether this flexibility has contributed to difficulties around giving and finance in world mission relationships, particularly with churches in the Majority World.

Changing patterns of giving and receiving

6.4   The biggest change in the pattern of giving and receiving in terms of personnel is expressed through the large number of short-term mission visits[95] that now take place through the Mission Agencies and the Diocesan Companion Links. Visits are a vital and necessary expression of relationship, and presence is a highly valued gift for all parties. Various types of visit take place as part of Diocesan Companion Links from the level of episcopal to parish visits with many combining both. Teachers' and young people's visits are also significant occasions for exposure to different cultures and professional development. The particular ministry of the Archbishop of Canterbury is a major expression of giving and receiving as he focuses on visits to churches in vulnerable contexts. The Mission Agencies also have specialist knowledge in short-term mission visits. USPG operates the Experience Exchange Programme and the Expanding Horizons scheme which focus on exposure, learning and exchange. They also send longer-term Mission Companions who serve for between two and six years approximately. CMS operate the Encounter Mission Community which provides opportunities for short-term visits based on cultural immersion or exposure for between four and six weeks. CMS also operate a longer-term mission partner scheme as well as the Timothy Fund which funds mission personnel from churches that previously received missionaries from the West. Other PWM Agencies such as Crosslinks and CMJ also operate long- and short-term mission schemes. The giving of money is a major expression of partnership relationships across the Anglican Communion. Donations or loans can be channelled through the Mission Agencies and the Diocesan Companion Links and increasingly through churches and smaller Mission Agencies.

6.5   There is often a direct link between a short-term mission visit and the raising of funds for projects or people in the countries visited. Many short-term mission encounters take place within a long-term mission relationship such as a Companion Link. In this context appropriate cross-cultural preparation can be provided which draws on long-term experience. Equally, Diocesan Companion Links and other styles of links use the extensive experience of the Mission Agencies to prepare those embarking on short-term mission visits. This sharing of expertise is an important aspect of co-operative working and needs to become common practice.

6.6   For many in the Church of England one of the immediate responses following a short-term visit is to raise money for the churches visited. Few, if any, who visit from the West can fail to be moved by the life and vitality as well as disturbed by the level of need in Majority World churches. This creates a desire to respond from those with the material resources in the West. This is a natural response as Christians see their fellow Christians in different parts of the world struggling to provide basic needs for themselves and their families. The generosity engendered

---

95 For further information about short-term mission see the 'Global Connections Code of Best Practice for Short-Term Mission 2012' at www.globalconnections.co.uk/code.

here is to be welcomed. A short-term visit can create great enthusiasm for mission and thankfulness for the generous hospitality received on the visit as well as a vision for future action. However, it is particularly important to listen and plan carefully at this point to avoid attitudes that reflect an 'us and them' mentality or 'us doing something for them'. The key issue for Church of England partners is how we look and listen to other cultures wisely and accurately. Care has to be taken to ensure the Western partner is seeing and anticipating need correctly. Would it be more accurate to use the term 'pilgrimage' rather than short-term mission visit? A pilgrimage is a journey with a spiritual purpose. There is an equality and mutuality in pilgrimage with elements of receiving and giving that may more accurately describe the experience of short-term mission.

Giving goods and equipment

6.7   Giving of goods and equipment is another way that Agencies, Companion Links and others have provided resources as a way of expressing relationships in the Body of Christ. As with donations of money, particular cultural intelligence and sensitivity is required when giving in this way. While gifts of computers or washing machines or cars may seem appropriate to Western Christians, in very different cultural contexts they may not be appropriate because of limited basic resources such as electricity. Listening and learning with cultural awareness and sensitivity are essential before embarking on projects. Many of the Mission Agencies have a long history of giving in this way. A major part of the overseas ministry of SPCK, for example, has been the donation of books to those in theological training and to clergy.

Accountability

6.8   Accountability is arguably the most difficult issue in giving internationally. Cultural norms and understandings differ and can be the cause of misunderstanding that may threaten the sustainability of relationships. Whatever channel is used to give money or goods to partners in the Majority World, those who are making large donations from the West are governed by charitable giving and accounting law which require accounts and reports to be kept as public record. Accountability for funds given and received as understood in the cultural and legal terms of the highly bureaucratized West can be experienced as lack of trust to those in communally based cultures in the Majority World. The means by which the societies of Western nations build and ensure trustworthiness in financial matters is at the same time the means by which our partners in the Majority World perceive a lack of trust in their cultural norms. This is particularly so as the Church of England uses terms like partnership, companionship and friendship to speak of world church relationships when these words signal different concepts in financial matters for those in communally based societies such as Africa and Asia.[96] The sometimes painful and unintended consequences of cultural difference call upon all parties to listen, seek to understand and forgive where necessary. These issues take careful explanation and understanding if they are not to disrupt cross-cultural relationships.

6.9   The nature of financial exchange differs greatly between a personal gift given in an individual capacity and a financial gift given by a church, Agency or other institution. For example, a gift is a very different means of financial exchange to a loan in the West. The differences may

---

96 See Maranz, *African Friends and Money Matters*, SIL International, 2001, pp. 38–40.

not be as clear in other cultures. Consequently, accountability is a very different matter with different types of donation. Issues surrounding accountability touch on the most sensitive aspects of culture in giving and receiving. Accountability, however, is not only a financial issue but a theological issue. All will be called to give account before God (Romans 14.12; Hebrews 4.13; Matthew 12.36). Financial accountability has to be seen as part of our accountability to God through being accountable to one another. The theological understanding of accountability is in the context of the love of God in the Body of Christ and has to be seen as part of our participation in God's mission. Part of this participation is to persevere in finding ways in which accountability can be understood and practised across cultures where each partner is able to understand and learn from the other and see the strengths and weaknesses in different cultures.

6.10   The influence of a colonial history has a profound effect on this issue of finance and accountability. Maranz says,

> 'during the colonial period African leaders were not accountable to the people under them but to their colonial masters. These in turn were accountable only to their home governments. The local people were there to be controlled, not informed. Surely this colonial pattern left indelible marks across the continent.'[97]

These are the contexts in relationships with partners in Africa and other parts of the Majority World that have to be taken into account when addressing complex financial issues.

Dependency

6.11   Can money be given without the receiver becoming dependent on a particular source? Dependency can destroy human dignity. The American theologian Glenn Schwartz[98] says,

> 'dependency syndrome has little to do with wealth or poverty. It has to do with the mentality on the part of both local people and the outsiders who try to help.'

Involvement in world mission relationships means asking deep questions about attitudes to receiving. Dependency will invariably arise in a relationship where there is also a sense of superiority on the part of the one partner. Is one of the vestiges of colonial attitude an unconscious sense of superiority on the part of the partner from the affluent West and in this case the Church of England? Mutuality in partnership will not be achieved if these uncomfortable questions are not faced and, if present, become the reason for repentance. One way in which dependency can be avoided is to allow partners in the Majority World to give gifts of money or goods to their partners in the Church of England. While this may be a cause of embarrassment for some in the materially rich West, giving can never be separated from receiving. Giving and receiving concerns human dignity at a fundamental level. Furthermore, we are all receivers first and foremost as we receive all that we have from God. As David says at the completion of the First Jerusalem Temple,

> 'But who am I and who are my people that we should be able to give as generously as this? Everything comes from you, and we have given you only what comes from your hand.' (1 Chronicles 29.14 NIV)

---

97 Maranz, *African Friends*, p. 39.
98 Schwartz, *When Charity Destroys Dignity: Overcoming Unhealthy Dependency in the Christian Movement*, Authorhouse, 2007.

6.12   Western partners receive from their partners in the Majority World in very different ways. While money is a tangible mode of exchange it is in the area of spirituality and community that Western partners receive most. English Anglicans visiting their partners in the Anglican Communion often experience communities with a very high degree of internal resilience in the face of conflict and natural disaster for example.

6.13   The foundational work of Marcel Mauss[99] in the fields of sociology and anthropology charts the nature of transfers and how they work in indigenous communities in Scandanavia, Polynesia and North America. His conclusion was that there is no such thing as a free gift. The giving of gifts or exchange of money, goods and people will always involve other obligations and transactions. World mission relationships from the West to Africa, Asia and Latin America are often expressed in terms of giving money, people and goods where it is unclear how the recipients will be able to give in return or to what level of gift giving they will be able to return. This is especially complex when Western Christians find it difficult to articulate their needs. This is a crucial area that needs focused attention if relationships are to move beyond dependency into genuine mutuality.

6.14   There is also the complexity of living in very different systems of economic redistribution. The West exercises a market economy system whereas in many parts of the Majority World the economic system will be that of gift exchange. In the market economy distribution and redistribution is carried out in institutional form by the state and other organizations. In a system of gift exchange such redistribution will take place at a much more personal or familial level.[100]

6.15   Of the giving of gifts from the West to Africans Maranz comments,

'Relationships are supposed to be mutually dependent, but if the Westerner is always the giver, a basic requirement of the system cannot be met. There really will never be reciprocity. The Westerner will never be in a position to be on the receiving end, as his or her material needs will never be greater than those of the borrower.'[101]

If obligations cannot be met, this can lead to a loss of status and self-esteem that is damaging to the relationship. Given that current practice in making financial transaction of various sorts is set against a historic inequality, developing relationships of mutuality, hospitality and partnership are highly challenging.

6.16   At this point partner churches need to look at the roots of their unity rather than differences in culture as the place where partnership, mutuality, hospitality and participation are found. As was discussed in Chapter 2, our common roots are found in mutual partnership and participation in the mission of God in the world where all Christians stand in equality as God's partners from all cultures. Likewise there is a need to understand different ways of understanding cultural norms in gift giving and financial exchange. This discussion now turns to a biblical example of financial exchange.

---

99 Mauss, *The Gift*, W.W. Norton, 1990 (first published 1950).
100 Maranz, *African Friends*, p. 70.
101 Maranz, *African Friends*, p. 70.

The Jerusalem collection

6.17   How can the biblical witness inform our practice of giving and receiving in the context of world mission? As part of his apostolic ministry, Paul initiates a collection for the church in Jerusalem following periods of great hardship and famine (Romans 15.26; Acts 21.20–24; 24.17; 1 Corinthians 16; Galatians 2.10). In Paul's sometimes difficult relationship with the church in Corinth the issue of the collection for the Jerusalem church initially became a cause of concern and later for reconciliation. In 2 Corinthians 8—9 Paul gives the clearest exposition of the place of giving and receiving in God's economy. He outlines a number of key points that can guide the church today in our receiving and giving in the context of world church relationships. Below are some learning points that arise from this biblical example.[102]

1. Paul uses the great generosity of the Macedonian churches (Philippi, Thessalonica and Berea) to urge the Corinthians to be generous. He makes the point that even though they were poor and themselves suffered much hardship and persecution, they 'begged us most insistently, and on their own initiative, to be allowed to share in this generous service to their fellow Christians' (2 Corinthians 8.4, Revised English Bible). The Macedonian churches gave beyond their means as they gave themselves to God and to the service of the church. In the case of such poverty and hardship it may have been tempting for the Macedonian churches to ask why the collection was not being made for them. This, however, is not the case. The Philippian church was known for its generosity as Paul himself had received a gift from it while in prison as well as a visit on behalf of the church from Epaphroditus. This was the only gift he received from the churches in the region. Giving and receiving is about dignity and discipleship. While Christians in the financially rich West may feel uncomfortable receiving financial or other gifts from those who are poorer, it is important that such gifts are given and received in the Spirit of God's generosity to his people. It is this that builds equality and mutuality. The scale of the gift may be different but the acts of giving and receiving have a profound effect on relationships. The parable of the Widow's Mite is evidence of this (Mark 12.41–44). There is a desire among many churches in the Majority World to give as part of their discipleship in the Body of Christ and, as with the Macedonian churches, this must be received in the spirit in which it is given. For the Western church there is a learning curve to be experienced in receiving and in articulating needs.

2. The Corinthian church was situated in a major city which was a centre of trade and exchange. It had many resources. However, despite Paul's earlier encouragement to it to give regularly and deliberately to the collection, resistance to his requests had grown among the congregation. Paul challenges this resistance through the example of Christ and by 'putting your love to the test' (v 8). He appeals to its love, in other words to its highest calling in Christ. He also urges it to complete what it started in that same spirit of love. Giving involves responsibility to others and needs to be completed at a point or stage agreed by all parties. Giving and receiving is about commitment which is part of our love in the Body of Christ. This also provides an example of giving and receiving financially as an expression of a deeper relationship.

3. Giving and receiving is an expression of the interdependence and partnership in the Body of Christ. Paul writes: 'At the moment your surplus meets their need but one day your need may be met from their surplus. The aim is equality' (v 14). The difference in global economics makes it difficult to see this interdependence and partnership through the giving and receiving of material gifts. However, money is only one way of expressing relationships in the Body of

---

102 This section was inspired by Ayodeji Adewuya's *A Commentary on 1 and 2 Corinthians*, SPCK, 2009.

Christ. There are many others such as friendship, mutual support and sharing of skills as well as prayer and worship. It is this which distinguishes a donor/recipient relationship from a relationship experiencing the deeper levels of participation and hospitality in God's mission.

4. Paul wants to ensure proper accountability and transparency where this collection is concerned. 'We want to guard against any criticism of our handling of these large sums; for our aims are entirely honourable, not only in the Lord's eyes but also in the eyes of men and women' (vv 20–21). Paul covers himself by the involvement of Titus and the two unnamed leaders in the churches in the collection and delivery of the funds. This biblical example of accountability shows the need for transparency in financial matters within the Body of Christ. Without this, unity in Christ is potentially compromised. Transparency and trust in relationships exist alongside each other and build each other.

5. The collection for the Jerusalem church is a cross-cultural enterprise. Paul collects the funds from the churches in the Gentile world to give to the Jerusalem church. That transaction is not without its complexities. First, Paul is treated with some suspicion by the Jerusalem church (Acts 21) and, second, there was a question as to how it would receive a gift from the Gentile Christians (Romans 15.31). However, for Paul, it is important to pursue despite all these difficulties,

> 'demonstrating to the Gentile churches that they are part of the same family as the Jewish Christians in Jerusalem and, still more important, demonstrating to the Jerusalem church that those strange Gentiles ... are fellow members with them in God's renewed people'.[103]

The possibilities for misunderstanding are plenty. However, it is worth all the effort of moving between cultures so that interdependence and partnership can be established under the Lordship of Christ.

6. 'Such generosity will issue in thanksgiving to God' (9.11); the ultimate end of all our giving is to give thanks to God in a cycle of giving generously that is ongoing and joyful. God blesses the church with abundance in Jesus which causes all members of the Body of Christ to respond with love and generosity to God through giving in many different ways to each other. Recognizing when one part of the Body of Christ is in need another part responds and brings glory to God and joy to all.

> 'If one part suffers, every part suffers with it; if one part is honoured, every part rejoices with it.' (1 Corinthians 12.26 NIV)

Likewise, no part of the Body of Christ can say to another part, 'I have no need of you'. (1 Corinthians 12.21 NRSV)

The collection for the church in Jerusalem provides a rich resource for study and reflection confirming aspects of giving and receiving already informing current practice and opening up new possibilities.

6.18   Giving and receiving is always to be seen as part of an ongoing process of praise and worship. What has been the effect of living in relationships characterized by asymmetry where one partner has money, goods and skills and the other the resources of community and spirituality? This is a vast simplification but serves to remind all that this is a journey towards mutuality, participation in God's mission and learning through genuine hospitality.

---

103 Wright, *Paul for Everyone: 2 Corinthians*, SPCK, 2003, pp. 84–5.

6.19   As the church in the West, including the Church of England, faces the spiritual crises of cultures facing the emptiness of consumerism and the long-term and deep effects of the global economic crisis fuelled by excessive consumption, attempts at supremacy are tenuous to say the least. The Western churches are moving, or arguably being pushed, to a new era of humility where it becomes essential to our survival that we learn the ways of community resilience from those in other parts of the world. Indeed, just as we are realizing we need to work at our past shapes of relationships, so we may find ourselves needing to deal urgently with the present realities of a global economic system with former mission regions such as China, India and Brazil becoming the economically powerful.

Affirmations

The Church of England, through the Mission Agencies and the Diocesan Companion Links, affirms:

- Its participation in the journey with partners in the global church in developing understandings of mutual giving and receiving that move beyond past patterns of dependency.

- Its continuing ministry, through the Mission and Development Agencies and the Diocesan Companion Links, of deepening our world church relationships expressed through worship and prayer, visits, financial and other means support of churches in the Anglican Communion and others in need.

Commitments

The Church of England, through the Mission Agencies and Diocesan Companion Links, commits to:

- Engagement in processes of developing greater cross-cultural understanding in financial and other means of donation.

- Exploring in its own life how to develop greater transparency in world church relationships. (The Mission Agencies and Companion Links hold great expertise in this area. See Resources for further contact details.)

Chapter 7

Becoming Cross-cultural Christians

Summary

This chapter begins with the understanding that the mission and ministry of the Church of England takes place in a multi-cultural context. In order to meet the challenges of the local context in England it will be argued that Christians in the Church of England need to develop a greater awareness of their place in the global church through understanding themselves as cross-cultural Christians. It will suggest ways in which dioceses and parishes can develop their cross-cultural awareness. It explores the place of the Church of England in the global fellowship of Anglicans as well as being part of the Body of Christ throughout the world.

Jesus Christ – our unity and our head

7.1   The church worldwide is a community of vibrant, life-giving and life-enhancing diversity which embraces many different cultures and contexts. It has done so throughout its history. The earliest church in the book of Acts shows the energy and vibrancy of its life in Jesus Christ which sustained it for the enormous challenges it faced. The sense of unity in the fast-growing early church was summarized theologically by Paul and Peter in the Epistles.

The Epistle to the Romans (10.12 New American Standard Bible) says,

> 'For there is no distinction between Jew and Greek for the same Lord is Lord of all, abounding in riches for all who call on Him, for whoever will call on the name of the Lord will be saved.'

Equally in the Epistle to the Ephesians (1.22 NASB) it says,

> 'He put all things in subjection under His feet, and gave Him as head over all things to the church, which is His body, the fullness of Him who fills all in all.'

The Body of Christ (1 Corinthians 12) is perhaps the most significant image of unity and diversity. It is adopted in Ephesians (2.19–22 NASB) to stress oneness in Christ,

> 'So then you are no longer strangers and aliens, but you are fellow citizens with the saints, and are of God's household, having been built on the foundation of the apostles and prophets, Christ Jesus himself being the cornerstone in whom the whole building being fitted together is growing into a holy temple in the Lord in whom you also are being built together into a dwelling of God in the Spirit.'

7.2   The image of God's household built upon the cornerstone of Jesus Christ works with that of the Body of Christ. A household is a community gathered in one place, which was one of the earliest expressions of the communities of followers of Jesus Christ. The household image, as with the body, concerns the relationship of the head, Jesus Christ, to the whole body and the relationship of the parts of the body or members of the household with each other. These images reflect the interdependence of God's church under Christ.

7.3   From the very earliest church the household of God has embraced diversity and has crossed cultures. The sign of the coming of the Holy Spirit (Acts 2) was an understanding of the message of Jesus as Messiah in the language of all of those assembled in Jerusalem for the feast of Pentecost. Pentecost was a multi-cultural and cross-cultural gathering. God's mission through the Holy Spirit has always been and is today about breaking down barriers erected by human beings and human systems. Following Pentecost, the story of the Book of Acts is about the cross-cultural journey undertaken by the Jewish believers who formed the earliest church as they grasped the vision of the extent of God's love for all peoples as expressed in Jesus Christ. This was a big, expansive vision and it took some struggles, conflicts and hurdles to embrace it and to draw others into awareness of it. Peter, Paul and the other apostles were the carriers or bearers of the vision. In the Epistles at times when the churches that they established throughout the known world were tempted to retreat into internal matters and to claim the gospel for their own so Paul, Peter and other writers challenged such limited vision by pointing to Jesus Christ, and the generous love of God (2 Corinthians 8–9 and the Jerusalem collection).

7.4   Throughout Christian history there have been times when the Holy Spirit enables the church to see anew the extent of God's love in Christ for all people in all places and their place in that global vision. Is the Church of England at such a moment now?

7.5   The shift in the focus of global Christianity, discussed in Chapter 1, away from the global North and West to the Majority World is described by Andrew Walls as follows,

> 'Christianity, once the religion of confident technological advance and rising affluence, and sometimes seeing these things as a mark of God's favour, is replaced by a Christianity that will increasingly be associated mostly with moderately poor and very poor people, and with some of the poorest countries on earth. And peoples from the non-Western world will be the principal agents of Christian mission across the world.'[104]

7.6   What are the implications of this shift for the churches in the Western world including the Church of England? First, there is a significant change in patterns of mission exchange away from the West to the Rest to from everywhere to everywhere. Significant numbers of Christians from the Majority World are now coming to the countries of the West, including England, from Africa, Asia and Latin America. If the dominant nineteenth–twentieth-century mission pattern is from the rich to the poor then the pattern in the twenty-first century is from the poor to the rich.

7.7   Second, many Christians from the Majority World who come to these islands join migrant churches which are becoming increasingly aware of the prompting of God's Spirit to be in mission to the whole community rather than only to their own migrant community. Therefore, it is becoming increasingly important for the indigenous churches in England to build relationships with the migrant churches which live, worship and minister here. English resistance to different styles of worship and faith of the migrant churches significantly limits opportunities for dialogue and sharing discipleship. Here is an example of cross-cultural mission at home which could prove

---

104 Walls, 'The Ephesian Moment in Worldwide Worship', in Farhadian (ed.), *Christian Worship Worldwide*, Eerdmans, 2007, p. 36.

to be a significant development for mission in England as well as strengthening links with churches in other parts of the world.

7.8   How is the church in the West and particularly the Church of England going to respond to this new situation? Vethanayagamony points out three ways in which the church in the West might learn from this new situation. First, he says that the Western churches should recognize the change and as a result it should undergo a 'mental revolution' or a 'conceptual shift' which involves a 'new humility'.[105] Second, the churches in the West should realize that 'we are always the recipients as well as the agents of mission'.[106] He says,

> 'It is God's mission, and human involvement is always first as addressee and only then as agent.'[107]

It follows then, that the approach to mission for all Christians and churches is that of

> 'a bold humility or a humble boldness'.[108]

He concludes,

> 'Asian, Latin American and African influenced Christianity in all its diversity and contextuality can provide a model for reshaping religion and the Christian faith into a holistic undertaking in the Western world. However, the issue is whether the Western churches are ready to embrace the opportunity available at their doorsteps.'[109]

7.9   The developments outlined above show a changing world vastly different from the world dominated by Europe for so many centuries. While these are general comments on the new relationships between the churches of the West and the Majority World it is necessary to look at the particular place of the Church of England and its relationships in the Anglican Communion. For the last 300 or more years the Church of England, through the Mission Agencies, was the church that sent people and with them their expertise to many parts of what we now know as the Anglican Communion. Today the Church of England is increasingly becoming the receiver of mission from other parts of the Anglican Communion.[110] In the Anglican Communion there is an awareness of the Church of England as the church of origin of the Communion not least because of the nature of the ministry of the Archbishop of Canterbury as Primus inter Pares of the Anglican Communion and the Church of England. Relationship to the See of Canterbury is the central point of communion for Anglicans. Among many in the Anglican Communion there is a sense of thanksgiving for the historic generosity of the Church of England. However, there is also a desire to see a greater transparency on the part of the Church of England concerning the challenges the church faces in England. Though some relationships between parts of the Anglican Communion have been strained, equally the bonds of affection are strong and deepening in many places.

---

105 Vethanayagamony, 'Mission from the Rest to the West', in Kalu, Vethanayagomony and Kee-Fook Chia (eds), *Mission After Christendom*, Westminster John Knox, 2010, p. 68.
106 Vethanayagamony, 'Mission from the Rest to the West', p. 68.
107 Vethanayagamony, p. 68.
108 Vethanayagamony, p. 69.
109 Vethanayagamony, p. 65.
110 Evidence for this statement is that the Mission Agencies and the Companion Links have and continue to provide opportunities for ministers from all parts of the Anglican Communion to work in dioceses, parishes and other networks on the basis of long- or short-term commitments.

7.10   The work of the Mission Agencies and the Companion Links as well as numerous other links between parishes and schools play a significant role in sustaining the bonds of affection as do relationships between Bishops through the Instruments of Communion particularly the Lambeth Conference. The challenge to the Church of England concerns the possibility of negotiating a new and rich place within the Anglican Communion by being open to both receiving and giving the hospitality of others as equals in Christ. How can that be achieved? The approach advocated here is that of a growing awareness in the Church of England, particularly at parish level, of being cross-cultural Christians. This is one of the ways in which intensification or deepening of relationships may happen.

From global to local

7.11   With the enormous developments in communications, it is easier to be aware of our partners in churches in different parts of the world. Yet it also seems difficult for such awareness to make a difference to the lives of many parish churches across England. So, how can Christians adopt a cross-cultural awareness that enables genuine encounter which has the potential to enrich discipleship in the local church?

7.12   The most fruitful route to bring about change through cross-cultural encounter is to enable local churches in one culture to speak to local churches in another. In the experience of many this is where real change in perspectives happens that can enrich our understanding of what it means to be the Body of Christ. Local here, in Anglican understanding, can mean the local church as the diocese or the local church as the parish church. It is the local worshipping community that is entrusted with participating in God's mission in a particular locality. A theological understanding of holistic mission expressed in a particular context is at the heart of this process. Holistic mission encourages a varied and diverse expression of Christian witness. Another way to understand this exchange theologically is as prophetic dialogue.

7.13   One example of how local church can speak to local church is through considering the same questions in different contexts. Two churches, one from Central Africa and another from an English diocese were asked to describe the joys and challenges of being the church in their country. The responses to this question emphasized similar challenges which focused, among others, on supporting clergy and training lay ministers to respond to need as well as encouraging young people to be active in church. The joys expressed included seeing new people come to faith but whereas the numbers in the English context were small the numbers in the overseas context were large. Discussion followed as to the reasons for this in an atmosphere of genuine exchange and learning.

7.14   The process for cross-cultural dialogue outlined here adopts the concept of challenge and support. All groups need both internal and external challenge and support to grow and develop. Prayer, worship and using the Bible are vital parts of this process as are the life experiences and learning of all in the group.

7.15   It is easy to become focused on the local context to the exclusion of the global. However, there are important reminders in Anglican life and liturgy that the local finds meaning in its relationship to the global. The Anglican understanding of church and ministry holds a balance between the local and the global particularly through the ministry of the Bishop. In liturgy prayer and intercession, whether as individuals or as part of the gathered community, focus on God's world and its needs is vital to liturgical celebration.

Engaging in cross-cultural dialogue

7.16   Here is a process for engaging in cross-cultural dialogue at local church level. It can enable churches wanting to move to an encounter of genuine mutuality.

Approach

The values that are at the heart of cross-cultural encounter in a local church context are those of friendship and hospitality. This involves welcoming the stranger as a friend in the name of Christ and being open to all that they have to give. It also means giving support and, at times, challenge. It involves listening, speaking, sharing and valuing each other.

7.17   There is an African proverb which says, 'the stranger brings the sharper sword'.

Those from outside a particular context can bring new insights into another culture by asking simple yet profound questions such as: Why? In approaching cross-cultural encounter it is important to be aware of our own culture. Though this may seem a strange place to start, it is in fact the only place to start thinking about other cultures. While culture is diverse it also has sufficient areas of recognizable similarity to make it identifiable as a unity. It has been so easy for English Christians to see their culture as dominant or normative and fail to appreciate that English Anglican Christianity is only one way of being the church. There are many other ways of expressing church which are equally as culturally influenced. Christians in parish churches need to be engaged in processes to develop understandings of how and why church life is expressed as it is here. A recent resource to help English Christians to reflect on their faith in the context of English culture is *The Faith of the English*.[111] It includes resources for group reflection on Englishness and faith.

Listening and learning

7.18   Listening is a vital part of receiving and welcoming the guest into a new community. To listen is to take seriously all that the guest has to bring and is to welcome them into the heart of a community. To take time to listen is to honour the guest and invite them into the heart of the life of a church knowing that as the guest is welcomed it is as if Christ is welcomed (Matthew 26). It is important to make the conversation with the guest the centre of our attention.

7.19   At many points along this part of this process it is possible for both listening and learning to stop or close down. What are the dynamics that make this happen and how can it be avoided? One of the dynamics may be differences in cultural expression. Some cultures have a more direct method of address than in English culture and it is possible to mistake this for an inappropriate response. It may veer too far down the challenge part of the spectrum and not have enough support. It is important to bear this in mind and make allowances for these dynamics. The Archbishop of York offers a helpful cross-cultural insight when he says,

> 'Christians in Britain may be passionately committed to an ideal or a position, through our mind and our will and even our heart, but we detach our passion and surround it with careful and measured phrases so that it does not offend or frighten. Some of the voices

---

111 Rooms, *The Faith of the English Integrating Christ and Culture*, SPCK, 2011.

from Africa practise this detachment but where they come alive is when they plunge into heartbeat of the terror of war, the dragging ache of poverty.'[112]

7.20   It is important to make difference the beginning of the conversation not the end. All too often the phrase 'that won't work here' indicates that listening and learning has stopped and that there is nothing left to learn or engage with. Philip Thomas, a parish priest in the north of England, in an address to the PWM Conference in 2001[113] offered four understandings of how this process works. The first model is entitled 'declaratory' and is, Thomas says, 'the most basic of inter-cultural community where one community addresses another without recognition of any differences of perspective'.[114] This first stage in cross-cultural encounter would be characterized by partners speaking to each other but there would be little encounter or learning or potential for change. Thomas's second phase is 'developmental' which he describes as

> 'more to do with the way in which implications of a partnership are developed, objectives are set and tasks undertaken. It is possible not only for one party to recognize the needs of the other but also to see them predominantly from their own perspective.'[115]

At this point it is easy for the Western partner to assume they know what is appropriate in a particular situation and stop listening to the partner. Thomas warns that

> 'in a partnership … it is important to keep asking, "who set this agenda?" who invited them to do so? In whose interest does the agenda work?'[116]

The third, or dialogical, phase reveals a fading of distinctions of donor or recipient or other differences and involves a 'sense of meeting, of encounter and of give and take'. The fourth stage Thomas describes as 'double-swing' mode which is a relationship 'marked by mutuality and interchange' and the 'shape of both parties has been changed from self-contained circles into a new form'.[117]

7.21   The value of this set of models or modes is that it gives a framework for understanding a process and marks stages along the journey of cross-cultural encounter. This process begs some key questions. For example, is it always necessary to move through all of the processes in each encounter or can experience mean that engagement can consistently occur at an advanced level of dialogical or double-swing?

7.22   Thomas poses a key question which is

> 'the theological question ultimately addressed to any partnership must be, "how have you been changed as a result of your relationship with each other?"'[118]

This places change and transformation as the benchmark of cross-cultural relationships. One of the most effective way of engaging in cross-cultural dialogue is through storytelling and sharing of experience. This is when each participant brings a story of hope or a story of sorrow or a story that raises questions and asks the other for their insights. A storytelling circle can be a place of remarkable mutuality and deep encounter.

---

112 Wheeler (ed.), *Voices from Africa*, Church House Publishing, 2002, p. 136.
113 Thomas, 'How Can Western Christians Learn from Partners in the World Church?' *International Review of Mission*, vol. 92, 2003, pp. 382–92.
114 Thomas, 'How can Western Christians Learn', p. 385.
115 Thomas, 'How Can Western Christians Learn', p. 387.
116 Thomas, 'How Can Western Christians Learn', p. 388.
117 Thomas, 'How Can Western Christians Learn', p. 389–90.
118 Thomas, 'How Can Western Christians Learn', p. 390.

Reflection

7.23   There can be no learning without a process of reflection after listening. Questions focused upon the spectrum of challenge and support are vital. For example: 'What affirms our journey and what challenges it?' Another question is highlighted above: 'How have we been changed as a result of our relationship?' What insights did the guest bring that challenge and support? These are all important questions to consider in this part of the process together with many others. Reflection can be done through questions or through reflecting on certain biblical passages such as the Woman at the Well or the Good Samaritan in a cross-cultural context. The process of reading and studying the Bible together has its own power for transformation and change. One Bishop has remarked on the transformative effect this had at the 2008 Lambeth Conference. Other ways of reflecting are through art and music. Maintaining openness to difference and to the voice of the other is an essential part of this process.

New awareness and action

7.24   In any dialogue, it is only the host who can apply the insights, challenges and support that the guest brings to their situation. New awareness can result within a process of reflection and can shape attitudes and behaviour. These can be expressed as a new insight into a situation or a growing knowledge of how to deal with difficult situations in new ways.

7.25   One way of understanding this process theologically is as mission as prophetic dialogue.[119] Cross-cultural encounter is prophetic dialogue because it embodies and communicates a vision of God's purposes for all people in dialogue. Bevans roots dialogue in the nature of God as communion,

> 'God in God's deepest identity is a relationship, a communion.'[120]

In each encounter God's purpose for the unity of all creation and all peoples is communicated that points towards the image of the time when all peoples from all nations will stand before God's throne and worship him (Revelation 7.9). Bevans's image of prophetic dialogue is remarkably practical. He gives images or examples of prophetic dialogue as a teacher or a storyteller. Prophetic dialogue across cultures, however, is not an easy process. It is costly and demanding.

> 'Solidarity with the other are very muddy waters.'[121]

Indaba

7.26   Indaba is a method of community dialogue taken from Southern Africa which formed an important part of the process of the 2008 Lambeth Conference. It has since been applied to dialogue between different dioceses in the Anglican Communion through the Continuing Indaba

---

119 Bevans, *Mission as Prophetic Dialogue*, Orbis, 2011.
120 Bevans, *Mission*, p. 10.
121 Monica Vega of the Episcopal Church in the USA, working in South Africa with people whose lives are affected by HIV/AIDS. Delivered as part of an address at the Everyone Everywhere Conference, October 2011.

project.[122] The initial Pilot phase of Continuing Indaba is currently nearing completion and has involved the Dioceses of Derby and Gloucester. It is a way of understanding and appreciating difference within a local mission context. It embodies the concept that the global and the local are part of each other and one is discovered through the other. The purpose of Indaba in the Anglican Communion concerns:

- Intensifying relationships across the Communion.
- Energizing local and global mission.
- Enabling genuine conversation across difference.

7.27   The purpose of the Indaba conversations is described like this:

'Continuing Indaba Conversations bring together diverse dioceses in order to hear the agenda and issues of each conversation partner with equal status and as mission partners across diversity. Participants will be women and men, lay and ordained, who are actively participating in local mission. The participants will encounter each other's mission context and engage in facilitated conversations across difference.

The participants will go back into their dioceses, their communities in general and into the wider world, able to share their experience of conversation across difference. This is the purpose of the Project – the participants are actually engaging in the issues of mission with one another, which leads on into action. The sign of success for this Project will be renewed energy for local mission in the dioceses strengthened by partnerships that have engaged in conversation across difference towards the common purpose of mission.'[123]

The Church of England can learn from the experience of the Dioceses of Derby and Gloucester concerning their involvement in Continuing Indaba and how the process could be adapted for wider use.

From the global to the local

7.28   The purpose of this focus on becoming cross-cultural Christians is about deepening the understanding of ourselves in the Church of England as global Christians. This is in order to experience in a deeper way the richness of being part of the Body of Christ as we bring our own gifts and experience and receive the same from others. It is in order that more of the Church of England can experience and be enriched by the church in other parts of God's world and so enrich its local mission. This is the movement between the global church and the local church which is essential for the development of our own local life and mission. In seeing ourselves as part of a global church which is growing and where the lives of whole communities are being changed and enriched so we are energized for local mission. To fail to see ourselves in this way is to cut ourselves off from the life and energy of the Body of Christ in all its variety and diversity and to be quickly overwhelmed by the challenges that the church faces. Through encounter with the global church we can come to see ourselves in a new way and be transformed in the life of Christ.

---

122 www.continuingindaba.org.
123 www.continuingindaba.org.

7.29   As well as sharing in the joys of the gospel we enter into deeper relationship through the sharing of sufferings. If one part of the Body of Christ suffers then all suffer. A mark of deepening relationships is the sharing in the pain of suffering and persecution even from afar. Paul describes this process,

> 'For just as we share abundantly in the sufferings of Christ, so also our comfort abounds through Christ. [6] If we are distressed, it is for your comfort and salvation; if we are comforted, it is for your comfort, which produces in you patient endurance of the same sufferings we suffer. [7] And our hope for you is firm, because we know that just as you share in our sufferings, so also you share in our comfort.' (2 Corinthians 1.5–7 NIV)

When one part of the body suffers so all suffer and when one part rejoices so all can rejoice. This is the essence of partnership in the gospel to which the Church of England has aspired for so long. The Church of England is not starting this process from nothing. Many in the Church of England are a part of the sharing of joys and suffering. However, there is still a journey to be made.

Affirmations

The Church of England at national, diocesan, parish and network level affirms:

- Its place in the global church of Christ, sharing its participation in God's mission within the Anglican Communion and with ecumenical partners worldwide.

- The need for further intensification and development of relationships across the global church in order to enrich participation in God's mission in the world.

- The development of processes at diocesan and parish level to enhance local mission through global engagement.

Commitments

- The use of Continuing Indaba and similar processes to build relationships with the global church at diocesan and parish level.

- The gathering of a database of resources for use in dioceses and parishes for developing awareness of being cross-cultural Christians.

Priorities for the Future

The purpose of our world mission relationships is to share in our common calling to participate in God's mission in the world. In order to fulfil that calling there is a need to **encourage** and to **enable** each other to proclaim the good news of Jesus Christ in and for the world. Our partnerships are a rich source of God's life and blessing in this common calling.

What are the key priorities today for the Church of England in future world mission relationships? In the course of the consultation process for the preparation of this report the following priorities have emerged.

1. **An active awareness in parishes and deaneries of being part of the global church.** Our local mission is part of God's mission in the whole of creation. Our local mission is incomplete if we fail to recognize ourselves as part of God's global mission. The purpose of our partnerships is to build the Body of Christ in each place in order to fulfil our calling to participate in God's mission in the world. It is a priority for parishes and deaneries to understand our global partnerships as an essential part of our local mission (1 Corinthians 12.26).

2. **The delivery and support of integral mission (the Five Marks of Mission) in dioceses, deaneries and parishes.** For Anglicans integral mission is best understood through the Five Marks of Mission. Integral mission as expressed in the Five Marks of Mission holds together proclamation of the good news of Jesus and social action. They are two sides of the same coin and both are essential marks of God's mission. Word and deed are held together. For the Church of England the work of integral mission is carried out primarily in the dioceses, deaneries and parishes where ministries of sacrificial service and prophetic *diakonia* are exercised.

3. **The proclamation of God's love in Christ to all people.** Proclamation of the message of the good news in Christ is the heart of the calling of all God's church in all places. Proclamation and service go hand in hand. The Church of England is called to a faithful response to the ministry of evangelism together with openness to learning from the global church in this ministry.

4. **A commitment to honesty and transparency in our local and global relationships.** The character of relationships in the Body of Christ is based on love (1 Corinthians 13.4–7) which is described as honouring others, not self-seeking or being angered and rejoicing in the truth. These are the characteristics of relationships that all should work towards within the context of relationships across cultures in our global partnerships. Our partnerships will bear fruit as they embody the values of honesty and transparency.

All in the Church of England are invited to worship, work and pray towards the fulfilment of these priorities.

Recommendations

Chapter 2 – Partnership, Participation and Hospitality

Affirmations and commitments

The Church of England affirms:

- With joy, the partnership shared with the Provinces of the Anglican Communion as well as ecumenical partners in the worldwide church.

- The need for the General Synod to strengthen the processes through which it hears from and responds to the voices of the Provinces of the Anglican Communion.

The Church of England is committed to:

- A theological and spiritual journey of intensified relationship with the Provinces of the Anglican Communion and ecumenical partners focusing on mutual participation in God's mission through generous and practical hospitality.

- Listening and learning through world church relationships.

- Being open to hear the voices of the Provinces of the Anglican Communion as they bear upon the life and witness of the Church of England .

Chapter 3 – Partnership in Practice

Affirmations

As the Mission Agencies and Diocesan Companion Links of the Church of England we affirm:

- The contribution of each other to God's mission in the world and in particular its expression through the Anglican Communion.

- Our continuing need to listen to and learn from each other in a sustained process of engagement.

Commitments

As the Mission Agencies and Diocesan Companion Links of the Church of England we are committed to:

- Principles of partnership and participation between ourselves based on mutual trust and co-operation for the furthering of God's mission in the world and in particular its expression through the Anglican Communion.

- A continuation of the journey away from former patterns of dependency and towards greater mutuality between ourselves and our partners in the global church.

- Listening to and learning from each other in England and from our global partners.

- The distinctive approach of Anglicanism to world mission based on the sacraments, Scripture and episcopal leadership.

As the Mission Agencies of the Church of England we make commitment to:

- Our continuing journey together in mission asking 'What does it mean to live in Covenant today?

- Our continuing life as part of the Church of England and the Anglican Communion.

Recommendations

- That the dioceses of the Church of England and the Mission Agencies work together in partnership including the possibility of raising funds for one or more of the Mission Agencies.

- That the Church of England through the General Synod be reminded of the principle of the Second 5%. That is, if the first 5% of giving is to the parish and diocese, the Second 5% should be directed to the Mission Agencies.

- That attempts are made to draw Anglican Agencies and parishes which are not part of the formal ways of engagement in world mission into the ongoing discussion on paths to mutuality and to use the annual World Mission Conference for this purpose.

Chapter 4 – Mission and Development

Affirmations

The members of PWM, comprising the Anglican Mission Agencies and Diocesan Companion Links, affirm:

- The Five Marks of Mission as a means of embracing the complementary yet distinctive approaches to God's mission in the world.

- The establishment of the Anglican Alliance for Relief and Development as a means of co-operation and shared learning within the Anglican Communion as an expression of our participation in God's mission.

- The engagement of the Church of England in the ongoing ecumenical work of Christian Aid and other Agencies to tackle poverty and to embrace life in all its fullness.

Commitments

The members of PWM, comprising the Anglican Mission Agencies and Diocesan Companion Links commit to:

- Continuing dialogue and action between the Mission Agencies, Companion Links and the Christian-inspired Development Agencies on the role of the local church around the world in their respective work areas.

- Working through the Anglican Alliance for Relief, Development and Advocacy to assist partnership in areas of particular need.

- Developing understandings of mutuality in mission and development and recognizing the gifts received as well as those given.

Chapter 5 – Hearing from Our Partners

Affirmations

- The Church of England at national, diocesan, parish, Agency and network level affirms the importance of close and attentive listening in nurturing relationships across cultures as an expression of our communion in the Body of Christ.

Commitments

- The Church of England at national, diocesan, parish, Agency and network level commits to the process of listening across cultures using methods such as Indaba to facilitate such listening and learning.

Chapter 6 – Receiving and Giving

Affirmations

The Church of England through the Mission Agencies and the Diocesan Companion Links affirms:

- Its participation in the journey with partners in the global church in developing understandings of mutual giving and receiving that move beyond past patterns of dependency.

- Its continuing ministry, through the Mission and Development Agencies and the Diocesan Companion Links, of deepening our world church relationships expressed through worship and prayer, visits, financial and other means support of churches in the Anglican Communion and others in need.

Commitments

The Church of England, through the Mission Agencies and Diocesan Companion Links, commits to:

- Engagement in processes of developing greater cross-cultural understanding in financial and other means of donation.

- Exploring in its own life how to develop greater transparency in world church relationships. (The Mission Agencies and Companion Links hold great expertise in this area. See Resources for further contact details.)

Chapter 7 – Becoming Cross-cultural Christians

Affirmations

The Church of England at national, diocesan, parish and network level affirms:

- Its place in the global church of Christ, sharing its participation in God's mission within the Anglican Communion and with ecumenical partners worldwide.

- The need for further intensification and development of relationships across the global church in order to enrich participation in God's mission in the world.

- The development of processes at diocesan and parish level to enhance local mission through global engagement.

Commitments

- The use of Continuing Indaba and similar processes to build relationships with the global church at diocesan and parish level.

- The gathering of a database of resources for use in dioceses and parishes for developing awareness of being cross-cultural Christians.

Appendix 1

The Philippian Model

1. **Partners have a common purpose**

   A partnership depends upon a clear, common task in which all partners can be involved. When entering a partnership, the questions must be asked: What is the purpose of the partnership? Are the parties involved able to play their role in achieving the goal?

2. **Partners are of equal status**

   In a partnership both partners must have equality of status. There must be mutual respect. Partnership cannot work where there are feelings of inferiority or superiority on either side. When entering a partnership, the questions must be asked: Are all ready to forego feelings of superiority? Do all have confidence to know they are as important as those with whom they are in partnership?

3. **Partners have a common basis of belief**

   Absolute theological parity is not a requisite for partnership, but a common basis of belief and a shared theological language within which to discuss our relationship in partnership is of vital importance. When entering a partnership, the questions must be asked: Do all have a basis of shared values and beliefs? Do all have a shared theological language with which to discuss both unity and diversity?

4. **Partners have a concern for unity in one another's community**

   Partnership between two groups depends upon each group being united. Unity is forged by humility. Without unity the partnership will be between parties within one or both of the groups, and will encourage division. It is the responsibility of each partner to encourage unity in the other, and, when appropriate, to offer services of reconciliation and not judgement. When entering a partnership, the questions must be asked: Is each partner prepared to seek the way of humility to unity? Are all committed to unity within their partner community?

5. **Partners are eager to communicate and to be with one another**

   Partners will seek ways to be in communication, using whatever means are available, but never neglecting personal visits. The purpose of the visits is for mutual encouragement and to discover how the partnership is proceeding. When entering a partnership, the questions must be asked: Is each community able to put in the resources of finance, time, and effort into visiting their partners and welcoming them into their homes and churches? Are all prepared to maintain the links by using all forms of communication available?

6. **Partners share complementary resources and skills**

   Partners will have complementary gifts and resources to share. Money will often be part of this, but money cannot dominate the relationship. Other gifts are required from both parties. The richer party must be prepared to offer more than money and neither side can take power over the other by the giving of gifts. When entering a partnership, the questions must be asked: How can money be placed in its correct context? How are the riches of the variety of gifts of all to be shared?

7. **Partners share in one another's struggles and victories**

   Partners will be prepared to share in liability and rejoice in one another's success. Partnership requires commitment that may, at times, lead to suffering in solidarity. It requires the ability to rejoice in the partner's success. When entering a partnership, the questions must be asked: Is each prepared to share in the suffering of the other? Are all prepared to share delight in victories?

   Revd Canon Dr Philip Groves

PWM General Secretaries Meeting 6 March 2003

COMMON MISSION

A Covenant

Mission Agencies of the Church of England

A common future

Over the last few years the Mission Agencies have been growing together within the framework of the Church of England's Partnership for World Mission (PWM). Historically these Agencies have been the primary contributors on behalf of the Church of England to the founding and expansion of the worldwide Anglican Communion. Such Agencies remain a major channel for on-going mission relationships and grassroots initiatives within the Communion. There are growing numbers of public issues and debates where the Agencies need to be more visible and where their contribution needs to be heard. This calls for new ways of working together to speak with one voice and take joint action. It includes recognizing the developing role of the Archbishop of Canterbury as President of the Anglican Communion and new opportunities for closer working between the Archbishop and the Agencies.

A Common Vision

1. We believe in promoting confidence in the gospel and an understanding of mission that is holistic and evangelistic within the context of the Five Marks of Mission[124] of the Anglican Communion.

2. We believe that our task in proclaiming the Kingdom of God can only be undertaken in partnership and within the fellowship of the worldwide church.

3. We believe the church is God's instrument for mission and recognize and affirm the voluntary principle as a proven model for mobilizing and encouraging effective engagement.

---

124 1. To proclaim the Good News of the Kingdom. 2. To teach, baptize and nurture new believers. 3. To respond to human need by loving service. 4. To seek to transform unjust structures of society. 5. To strive to safeguard the integrity of creation and sustain and renew the earth. 6 March 2003

A Common Commitment

1. To increase co-operation while acknowledging the richness of our diversities.

2. To increase mutual support, discussion of common issues and the development of strategic co-operation through regular meetings of the General Secretaries.

3. To build up contact, regular meetings and working Links between the Archbishop of Canterbury and the General Secretaries of the PWM Agencies.

4. To ensure meetings of specialist staff to share concerns, models of good practice and engage in practical partnerships.

5. To issue agreed public statements, study and promotional materials on issues of common concern.

6. To consult as widely as possible on mission issues in the Anglican Communion and in collaboration with relevant commissions, working parties and networks authorized by the Primates Meeting and the Anglican Consultative Council.

Appendix 3

Partnership for World Mission Conference 2011

Shaping the Future

Preparing for the Conference

Introduction

At the 2010 World Mission Conference Bishop Chad Gandiya, Bishop of Harare, set out **seven Ingredients of True Partnership.** The Conference Planning Group believe that these seven Ingredients provide an invaluable resource for deeper thought and consideration in preparation for the 2011 Conference.

Participants at the 2011 PWM Conference are invited to use the following reflections to prepare for the conference. The reflections can be used in a number of ways. For example, they can be used as part of a daily personal reflection or devotional time either alone or with others or in a discussion group before the conference. They can be revisited after the conference to identify and record learning points.

These seven Reflections are designed to provide material for reflection for 7 days prior to the conference. The purpose is to reflect on our current practice of linking in order to deepen and develop such practice so that it more closely reflects cross-cultural partnership as one expression of being the Body of Christ. The 4-D process used throughout is based upon **Appreciative Inquiry** (AI). AI is defined as

> 'the co-operative search for the best in people, their organizations and the world around them. It involves discovery of what gives life of an organization or community when it is most effect and most capable in economic, ecological and human terms.'[125]

AI will be used as the process at the 2011 PWM Conference. It has been used in various contexts including one of the Anglican Mission Agencies to discern their future direction. It is about learning from an appreciative base and seeking new direction. It focuses on what energizes and gives life rather than concentrating on problem areas.

As you think and reflect make a note of any insights that occur and that could be shared at the conference. There will be an opportunity to share these with others at the conference and to use these to discuss them more widely in the conference workshops.

---

125 Cooperrider and Whitney, *Appreciative Inquiry, A Positive Revolution in Change*, Berrett Koehler, 2005, p. 8.

All participants need to have read Bishop Chad Gandiya's keynote addresses given at the 2010 PWM Conference. These can be found on the PWM Conference website accessed through www.churchofengland.org/our-faith/mission/worldmission/pwmconference.

Bishop Chad locates the current context for partnership in the shift in 'Christianity's centre of gravity to the non-Western world'. He quotes Prof. Andrew Walls who says that there have been three turning points in history. The first shift occurred in the first century when the early church moved from being an all-Jewish community to an overwhelmingly Gentile community. The second shift happened in medieval times when the centre for the church moved from the East and Southern Mediterranean to the north and west. The third shift is happening now when the centre of gravity of the church has moved from the North-West to Africa, Latin America and Asia.

7 Ingredients of True Partnership

Reflection 1

Compatibility and difference – 'In the Bible[126] partnership is only possible between parties which, while maintaining their individual identities, are nevertheless compatible with one another. In partnership there is no thought of one eclipsing the other's identity ... partnership accepts and celebrates the differences between the parties.'

> **Discovery** – How does engaging with difference energize a partnership you are involved in? Think of stories and examples where the partnership has grown as a result of engaging with difference and compatibility.
> **Dream** – Looking to the future where are the possibilities for growth in your partnership as a result of being open about your differences?
> **Design** – What are the values that guide you into a future of compatibility and difference in your partnership?
> **Deliver** – What resources do you envisage you will need to pursue your future? What hope will sustain that future?

Reflection 2

Specific and agreed vision – 'Partnership assumes a task or a mission can be better accomplished when two or more parties work together ... without a specific and agreed vision or task partnership would not make sense.'

> **Discover** – Think of the stories and examples when a specific and agreed vision or task has helped you to develop a partnership. What values have each partner in the partnership brought to the whole that has given it life and energy?
> **Dream** – What is your vision for the future of this partnership?
> **Design** – What do you see as the ideal vision for the partnership?
> **Deliver** – What are the changes you make now that will sustain you into the future?

---

126 The Epistle to the Philippians is a particularly rich source of insights on partnership. Read this short epistle and identify how compatibility and difference are worked through in the relationship between Paul and the Philippians.

Reflection 3

Mutually beneficial and not a one-sided affair – 'A relationship in which one party does all the giving and the other does all the receiving does not qualify to be called a partnership but perhaps a donor/recipient relationship.'

Bishop Chad tells the following story:

> 'Not so long ago a certain Christian leader came up to me and said, "You know we can help your diocese a lot. My diocese has a lot of money. Let us establish a partnership between our dioceses. When you get home send me an email with a list of projects you need financial assistance for. I don't doubt that he meant it but for me that was not the kind of relationship or partnership I wanted to establish between our dioceses and so I let it pass for a while. We met again a while later and he reiterated his offer and I suggested that his diocese made a donation to my diocese without going in to building a partnership relationship as our understanding of partnership was quite different.'

Discover – What are the positive aspects of this story?
Dream – What are the values of true partnership you can glean from this story?
Design – How can partnership express its true values in your current relationship?
Deliver – What changes need to occur for this to be fulfilled?

Biblical reflection – Read 2 Corinthians 8—9. Paul was writing to the Corinthian church to seek reconciliation as their relationship had been experiencing significant tensions. In chapters 8 and 9 Paul specifically urges it to continue to collect the gifts for his collection for the church in Jerusalem which was experiencing considerable hardship. Reflecting on these chapters consider the language that Paul uses to urge the Corinthian church to continue its giving. What does this say to us about giving and receiving financial gifts today.

Reflection 4

Partners must stay faithful to one another. 'Partnership is built on mutual trust and faithful commitment to one another. Unfortunately a lot of so called partnerships are built on suspicion and mistrust and as a result they do not last.'

Trust is the bedrock of any relationship. It takes time to build but can be broken in an instant. It is a most valuable commodity since without it any sense of working together is impossible. It can be difficult to build trust in cross-cultural partnerships as different cultural expectations can act like the proverbial elephant in the room – that which is never expressed openly but remains a powerful presence heavily influencing decisions and relationships. Trust anticipates certain behaviours that warrant the belief of another. For example loyalty and honesty create confidence which leads to trust. Building trust needs constant tending in cross-cultural relationships.

Discover – How have you been able to build trust in cross-cultural relationships? Give stories and examples to illustrate.
Dream – What is the purpose of cross-cultural relationships and what are we called to become through them?
Design – What possibilities open up when a high level of faithful commitment exists in cross-cultural relationships?
Deliver – How might you sustain your trust-based relationships?

Reflection 5

Mutual respect based on equality – 'Mutual respect is built on the foundation of equality between the partners.'

Bishop Chad uses the image of a football field to speak about the need for equality between partners as the basis of mutual respect. He says,

> 'Partnership in most mission organizations is a bit like this people's game but played on mountain slope pitches. The Mission Agencies' goal posts they are defending are at the top while those of the so called partners are at the bottom of the slope. Now you tell me who is going to win the game and why? There is no equality whatsoever between the two teams.'

Is the shift away from the power base of Christianity in the North and West (USA, Canada and Europe) towards Africa, Asia and Latin America beginning to level the football field?
What effect might this shift have on the need to build mutual respect based on equality in our partnerships?

> **Discover** – What have been the strengths of our current world mission relationships even though they have not been played on a level playing field?
> **Dream** – What might the level playing field feel like?
> **Design** – What are the factors that are influencing the shift to a level playing field?
> **Deliver** – What needs to happen so level the playing field?

Reflection 6

Financial transparency and making decisions together – 'Each partner needs to involve the other in decisions that can affect the partnership so that each can own the outcome. There is a need to go beyond the rhetoric of partners and partnership in mission.'

In this section Bishop Chad some of his most challenging comments about the way we conduct world mission especially in relation to money. He talks about the lack of transparency around financial decision making.

> 'Many so-called partners are directly or indirectly involved in raising funds from which they benefit but often are kept in the dark about how much has been raised and are not involved in deciding how those funds should be used. This raises a fundamental question. Whose resources are they in the first place? God's or ours?'

> **Discover** – Think of some examples of financial transactions in your world mission relationships. How have these given life to each partner?
> **Dream** – What are the ways of giving that build trust in world mission relationships?
> **Design** – What might be the most constructive way to approach financial giving given cultural differences?
> **Deliver** – What do we hope for in our financial giving and receiving?

Reflection 7

Maintaining partnerships – 'Partnership involves a process not an event. Therefore we have to recognize that partnerships may be more challenging to maintain than to start. Partnerships last when they stay focused on the ultimate goals, not immediate problems.'

Partnership is about relationship and is ongoing and needs careful nurturing. Partnership relationships need a number of horizons for their long-term health and life. The first horizon as Bishop Chad says is about ultimate goals. It is important for all parties to understand what we are working towards for both partners. The second horizon concerns friendship and hospitality as the modus operandi of God's mission. Relationships are conducted through receiving one another and the exchange of the gifts of friendship of which money is one part. The third horizon concerns immediate concerns and problems that can be shared as part of an on-going relationship. For example, a church undergoing persecution or where a disaster or emergency occurs. Maintaining a long-term relationship requires commitment and energy particularly with the demands of relationships across cultures.

> **Discover** – Looking over the history of partnerships you have been involved in what are the hallmarks of its life?
> **Dream** – What is the best you hope for in your continuing relationship?
> **Design** – What is your long-term shared vision for the partnership?
> **Deliver** – How can each party be empowered in the partnership?

Conclusion

When you have completed the reflections look back on the series and identify three or four points that you wish to bring to the conference. There will be a notice board for you to post your headline learning points and opportunities to contribute to discussions.

Appendix 4

The Future Shape of Partnership for World Mission

The main role of PWM has been to provide a Link between the Anglican Mission Agencies and the General Synod, to provide a focus for co-operation and sharing for the Mission Agencies, Diocesan Companion Links and others involved in world mission from an Anglican perspective. In addition, PWM is mandated to act as an advocate for Anglican world mission involvement in the wider ecumenical forums on world mission.

The results of consultation with the Agencies and dioceses over the last two years in the current process of searching for a coherent framework for world mission in the Church of England has revealed a consensus on the need for a light structure to provide a focal point for world mission concerns for the Church of England and to provide a structural link with the General Synod. For example, two Agency leaders have commented on the need for PWM as follows,

> 'PWM is a constant reminder that my Agency does not and should not work on its own. Without PWM we would not have the wider view of who we are and what our role is.' (Mission Agency General Secretary)

> Also, 'As a smaller Agency we need PWM to give a wider perspective that we belong together as Anglicans involved in world mission.' (Associate Agency representative)

Relationships with the General Synod

Many General Synod members are involved in the Mission and Development Agencies as well as their Companion Links and the many other ways in which the Church of England expresses its world mission relationships. Indeed several of the Mission Agency General Secretaries are members of General Synod. However, PWM provides a structure and therefore a coherent presence representing world mission in the Archbishops' Council as part of the Mission and Public Affairs Division. Without this an important voice would be lost that brings together the voice of the Mission Agencies and the Companion Links and is embedded into the life of the General Synod. The PWM structure is one that brings together diverse yet related voices characterized by the representation it enables through the Anglican Communion and World Mission Panel, the PWM General Secretaries Meeting, the annual meeting of the General Secretaries with the Archbishop of Canterbury and the annual World Mission Conference together with the work of the World Mission Policy Adviser. The Appointments Committee of the General Synod also appoints a representative from General Synod to the Governing Bodies of the Anglican Mission Agencies. This is also a structure which is embodied in the role formerly of the PWM Secretary and now of the World Mission Policy Adviser. The nature of the post holder at the heart of PWM is crucial to its effective working. This paper now turns to the future shape of the post.

The future of the PWM Post

Background

The current PWM post, the World Mission Policy Adviser, comes to an end in June 2012. Discussion on the feasibility of a continuing PWM post are ongoing at the time of writing and have occurred at the World Mission and Anglican Communion Panel and with the Mission Agency General Secretaries meeting of the full member Mission Agencies. The following issues have emerged.

1. The General Secretaries so far consulted have said that there is a job of co-ordination to be done between the Mission Agencies and the NCIs as well as the Church of England dioceses.

2. From the perspective of the NCIs/MPA a continuing role focused on co-ordination alone is not sufficient reason to hold a role devoted to world mission and the case for a strategic purpose beyond co-ordination would need to be made. Given limited resources in both the NCIs and the Mission Agencies, a jointly funded part-time (60%) or half-time post may be possible.

What is the job that needs to be done?

This Report on world mission relations argues that the changing role of the Church of England in world mission relationships will mean moving towards an approach characterized by mutual participation in God's mission. If this role is to be made a reality at diocesan and parish levels it will need a strategic focus. The main area that needs to be addressed is that as a church in mission in the UK there is a need to increase the capacity in the Church of England to learn from the church worldwide and to be transformed in its own life by such encounters.

Outcome

The desired outcome is an attitudinal change at all levels that increases the capacity of the Church of England to see itself as part of and learn from the church worldwide. This will require an envisioning process focusing on ordained and lay leaders of the Church of England of working with the world church both at home and in world mission relationships.

Apart from this focused approach the World Mission and Anglican Communion Panel together with the Mission Agency General Secretaries meeting will identify particular issues in world mission that need particular attention. The following areas have potential for strategic development:

- Relationship between mission and development and the respective Agencies.

- Funding streams to global partners.

- Relationship between home and overseas Mission Agencies.

- Developing relationships between Mission Agencies and Companion Links.

These are all areas where focused attention could result in strategic development to the Church of England and her Mission Agencies and Companion Links.

Changes to PWM structures

The last review of PWM took place in 2006. The main changes it brought about were the establishment of the Anglican Communion and World Mission Panel. This new body differed from the previous PWM Panel in that its membership has been widened to include all the partners in the Church of England's involvement in world mission. The functions are:

(a) In relation to the Archbishops' Council, General Synod and the Mission Agencies: to stimulate and encourage critical reflection and to advise on world mission issues and proposals in the light of the Christian understanding of our role in co-operating in God's Mission.

(b) On behalf of the Archbishops' Council: to be the principle link in world mission and Anglican Communion relationships concerns, on behalf of the Archbishops' Council, between the General Synod and

i.   The Anglican Consultative Council;
ii. The Church of England members serving on relevant Anglican Communion Commissions and Networks;
iii. Individual provinces and dioceses of the Anglican Communion and United Churches incorporating former Anglican dioceses.

(c) To provide a forum for information exchange in world mission and Anglican Communion relationships concerns.

(d) To promote collegiality and mutual support between Church of England members serving on Anglican Communion Commissions and Networks and Church of England bodies involved in world mission and Anglican Communion relationships concerns.

(e) To support the work of the Partnership for World Mission Office.

The Panel has provided an effective space for the dissemination of information and critical evaluation of practices in world mission. However, it has been uncertain about its role with regard to PWM in a time of review, evaluation and change. This has become particularly acute regarding applications from various Agencies in the Church of England and other Ecumenical Agencies for membership of PWM. It has been uncertain where responsibilities for these decisions lie. Legal opinion has revealed that further review of the World Mission and Anglican Communion Panel Constitution is necessary. This will form part of the work of the proposed new job description for the World Mission Policy Adviser.

PWM has in its membership focused exclusively on Mission Agencies. However, the place of Christian Development Agencies which see themselves as engaging in God's mission in the world and which work mainly with Anglican churches is much less clear. Should the parameters of membership of PWM be expanded to include Christian-inspired Development Agencies?

Conclusion

Given the increasingly diverse nature of involvement in world mission in the Church of England, it is widely agreed that there is a need for PWM to continue in some form. The question is, what form? The key issue is the shape of a continuing designated PWM post that combines necessary co-ordination with a sharp edge that will enable real change and development in cross-cultural working and awareness at diocesan and parish level. At the time of writing discussions are continuing to achieve this.

Diocesan Companion Links

Bath and Wells – Dioceses of Lusaka, Central Zambia, Northern Zambia, Eastern Zambia, and Luapula.

Birmingham – Dioceses of Lake Malawi, Southern Malawi, and North Malawi.

Blackburn – Dioceses of Bloemfontein (South Africa), and Braunschweig (Germany).

Bradford – North Sudan, South West Virginia (USA), and Erfurt (Germany).

Bristol – Uganda, and Meissen (Germany).

Canterbury – Madagascar, Arras (France), and Basel (Switzerland).

Carlisle – Madras (CSI), Zululand, Northern Argentina, and Stavanger (Norway).

Chelmsford – Dioceses of Embu, Kirinyaga, Mbeere, Meru of the Anglican Church of Kenya, Trinidad and Tobago, Karlstadt (Sweden), and Iasi (Romanian Orthodox).

Chester – Melanesia, Aru, and Boga (Congo).

Chichester – The Gambia, Sierra Leone, Liberia, Cameroon (through IDWAL), Nakuru, Nyahururu, and Kericho (Anglican Church of Kenya).

Coventry – Kaduna (Nigeria), and Syrian Orthodox Church in Jerusalem.

Derby – Church of North India (Ecumenical Link).

Durham – Lesotho, Alba Lulia, and North Elbia (Romania).

Ely – Vellore (Church of South India).

Exeter – Cyprus and the Gulf, Thika (Kenya), and Bayeaux and Lisieux.

Gloucester – Karnataka, Central Dornakal (Church of South India), Vasteras (Sweden), Western Tanganyika, and El Camino Real (ECUSA).

Guildford – Nigeria (IDWAL), Evry (Catholic Diocese of Paris), and Viborg (Denmark).

Hereford – Dar es Salaam, Masasi, Newala and Tanga (Tanzania), Zanzibar, and Nuremburg (Germany).

Leicester – Kiteto and Mount Kilimanjaro (Tanzania), Trichy-Tanjore (Church of South India), and Yokohama (Japan).

Lichfield – West Malaysia, Kuching (Singapore), Qu'appelle (Canada), Mecklenberg (Germany), and Matlosane (South Africa).

Lincoln – Ecumenical Link with Tirunelveli, and Tuticorin-Nazareth Dioceses (Church of South India).

Liverpool – Akure (Nigeria), and Virginia (ECUSA).

London – Angola, and Mozambique.

Manchester – Lahore, Namibia, and Tampere (Finland).

Newcastle – More (Norway), and Botswana.

Norwich – Papua New Guinea.

Oxford – Dioceses of Kimberley and Kuruman (South Africa), Vaxjo (Sweden), and Nandyal (Church of South India).

Peterborough – Bungoma (Kenya), Seoul (South Korea).

Portsmouth – Ghana, Nigeria, and Stockholm.

Ripon and Leeds – Colombo, and Kurunagala (Sri Lanka).

Rochester – Estonia, Dioceses of Mpwapwa and Kondoa (Tanzania), and Harare.

St Albans – Guyana, North East Caribbean and Aruba, Windward Islands, and Belize.

St Edmundsbury and Ipswich – Kagera (Tanzania).

Salisbury – Episcopal Church in Sudan, Evreux (RC France), and Latvia.

Sheffield – Argentina, and Hattingen-Witten (Germany).

Sodor and Man – Diocese of Cashel and Ossory (Church of Ireland).

Southwark – Manicaland, Central Zimbabwe, Matabeland, and Masvingo (Zimbabwe).

Southwell and Nottingham – Natal (South Africa).

Truro – Strangnas (Sweden).

Wakefield – Mara (Tanzania), Faisalabad (Pakistan), and Adelaide (Australia).

Winchester – Uganda, Myanmar, Rwanda, Burundi and the Congo, and Florence (Italy).

Worcester – Peru, Magdeburg (Germany), and Morogoro (Tanzania).

York – Cape Town, False Bay, Saldanha Bay (South Africa), Mechelen (Germany), Brussels, and Bungoma (Kenya).

Resources

The Anglican Mission Agencies all publish a variety of resources for use in parish churches.

Church Army

Operating as a society of Evangelists within the Anglican Communion, our mission is about sharing faith through words and action in order to make Jesus famous. Church Army works where the need is greatest – sharing the love of Christ to bring transformation to individuals and communities across the UK and Ireland. At the forefront of the new fresh expressions agenda, Church Army mobilizes around 500 evangelists and staff to reach out to people who have little or no connection with the church. Church Army Evangelists are admitted to the office of Evangelists within the Anglican Communion on behalf of the Archbishop of Canterbury and work under licence from the local Bishop. The society also helps discern the evolving mission of the church through the work of it's internationally respected research arm – The Sheffield Centre.

Wilson Carlile Centre, 50 Cavendish Street, Sheffield S3 7RZ, UK
Tel +44 (0)044 0300 123 2113
www.churcharmy.org.uk
info@churcharmy.org.uk

The Church's Ministry Among Jewish People (CMJ)

Our aims are to encourage Jewish people to come to faith in Jesus as their Messiah; to support them in serving Him as Lord in the light of God's purposes for them; and to equip the Church to be involved in this Mission.

Eagle Lodge, Hexgreave Hall Business Park, Farnsfield Notts NG22 8LS, UK
Tel +44 (0)1623 883960
www.cmj.org.uk

Church Mission Society

CMS is a community of 2,500 members committed to evangelistic mission, working to see our world transformed by the love of Jesus. Members commit to seven promises as they aspire to a whole lifestyle shaped by God's mission. CMS supports people in mission making disciples, resourcing leaders and transforming communities in over 35 countries in Africa, Asia, Europe, the Middle East and Latin America (CMS and the South American Mission Society integrated in 2010).

CMS, Watlington Road, Oxford OX4 6BZ, UK
Tel +44 (0)1865 787400
Fax +44 (0)1865 776375
 www.cms-uk.org, and www.wearesayingyes.org
info@cms-uk.org

Church Pastoral Aid Society (CPAS)

Since 1836, the mission of CPAS has been to enable people to hear and discover the good news of Jesus Christ. Research shows effective leadership is a primary factor in healthy, mission-focused churches. Over the next decade CPAS will be focusing on the development of leaders within churches, in order to help realize our vision of a Christ-centred, Bible-based, mission-focused church that reaches out effectively to local communities.

> Athena Drive, Tachbrook Park, Warwick CV34 6NG, UK
> Tel +44 (0)1926 458458
> www.cpas.org.uk info@cpas.org.uk

Crosslinks

Crosslinks is an international Mission Agency with its roots in the Bible and its principal sphere of operations in the worldwide Anglican Communion.

Our prime focus is making Christ known through the proclamation and teaching of God's Word in the power of the Holy Spirit. Founded in 1922 as BCMS, our slogan is 'God's Word to God's World'.

> 251 Lewisham Way, London, SE4 1XF, UK
> Tel +44 (0)20 8691 6111
> Fax +44 (0)20 8694 8023
> www.crosslinks.org

Intercontinental Church Society (ICS)

ICS is an evangelical Anglican mission to English-speakers of any nationality. We are a patronage society (recruiting ministers and often owning the buildings of international Anglican congregations abroad) and a mission to English-speakers through church growth, church planting and outreach to tourists. Areas of operation: Continental Europe and the Mediterranean. We also publish the Directory of English-speaking Churches Abroad.

> 1 Athena Drive, Tachbrook Park, Warwick, CV34 6NL, UK
> Tel +44 (0)1926 430347
> Fax +44 (0)1926 888092
> www.ics-uk.org

The Mission to Seafarers

A missionary society of the Anglican Church, The Mission to Seafarers serves seafarers of all races and creeds in 230 ports worldwide. We offer friendship, comfort in times of distress, spiritual support, counselling, help in cases of injustice and a welcome at our seafarers' centres.

> St Michael Paternoster Royal, College Hill, London, EC4R 2RL, UK
> Tel +44 (0)20 7248 5202
> Fax +44 (0)20 7248 4761
> www.missiontoseafarers.org

The Mothers' Union (International Work)

The Mothers' Union is a Christian organization promoting the well-being of families worldwide. With over one million members in 70 countries, we achieve this by developing prayer and spiritual growth in families, studying and reflecting on family life and marriage and its place in society and resourcing our members to take practical action to improve conditions for families, nationally and in the communities in which they live.

24 Tufton Street, London, SW1P 3RB, UK
Tel +44 (0)20 7222 5533
www.themothersunion.org

The Society for Promoting Christian Knowledge (SPCK)

The Society has three arms: Worldwide, Diffusion and Publishing. SPCK Worldwide distributes books and educational materials for Christians in ministerial training in some of the poorest parts of the world, free to the users.

SPCK Diffusion aims to produce innovative materials to reach a wide audience with information in a form relevant to their interests and experience.

SPCK Publishing produces a wide range of publications for both general and specialist readers.

SPCK, 36 Causton Street, London, SW1P 4ST, UK
Tel +44 (0)20 7592 3900
Fax +44 (0)20 7592 3939
www.spck.org.uk

United Society for the Propagation of the Gospel: Anglicans in World Mission (USPG)

USPG: Anglicans in World Mission exists to support the churches of the Anglican Communion as they engage in God's holistic mission. We are a major Anglican Mission Agency focused on sustaining relationships between churches and supporting our partners in growing the church's capacity for mission, particularly through leadership development and health work.

USPG, Anglicans in World Mission, 47–51 Great Suffolk Street, London, SE1 0BS, UK
Tel +44 (0)20 7921 2200
www.uspg.org.uk
enquiries@uspg.org.uk

The Associate Members of Partnership for World Mission

Bible Society

Stonehill Green, Westlea, Swindon, SN5 7DG, UK
Tel +44 (0) 01793 418222
contactus@biblesociety.org.uk

BibleLands

24 London Road West, Amersham, Bucks, HP7 0EZ, UK
Tel +44 (0)1494 897959
jeremy.moodey@biblelands.org.uk

Borneo Mission Association

3 Bishops Walk, Llangollen, Denbighshire, LL20 8RZ, UK
Tel +44 (0)1978 869379
ann@borneo-editor.fsnet.co.uk

Centre for Health and Pastoral Care

10 Sowerby Road, Thirsk, North Yorkshire, YO7 1HX, UK
Tel +44 (0) 1845 522580
www.holyroodhouse.freeuk.com/sitemap.html

Christians Aware

2 Saxby Street, Leicester, LE2 OND, UK
Tel +44 (0) 116 254 0770
barbarabutler@christiansaware.co.uk

Congo Church Association

8 Burwell Meadow, Witney, Oxon, OX28 5JQ, UK
www.congochurchassn.org.uk

Egypt Diocesan Association

5 Michel Lutfallah Street, Zamalek, Cairo, Egypt, 11211.
Tel +20 (2) 27380821/3/9
www.dioceseofegypt.org/english/support/eda

The Jerusalem and the Middle East Church Association

1 Hart House, The Hart, Farnham, Surrey, GU9 7HJ, UK
Tel +44 (0)1252 726994
Fax +44 (0)1252 735558
secretary@jmeca.eclipse.co.uk

Kenya Church Association

Revd Bryan Wadland, Secretary, 55 Copthall Road East, Ickenham, UB10 8SE, UK
Tel +44 (0)1895 613904
bryan@kenyachurchassociation.org

MANNA

Mozambique and Angola Anglican Association, St David's Rectory, Bettws Hill, Newport, S Wales, NP20 7AD, UK
Tel +44 (0)1633 857643
www.churchinwales/manna.org

Melanesian Mission

Dave Friswell, Executive Officer, 15 Covell Close, Bury St Edmunds, Suffolk, IP33 2HU, UK
Tel +44 (0)1284 701 988
mission@talktalk.net

Papua New Guinea Church Partnership

Louise Ewington, Director, St Andrew's House, 16 Tavistock Crescent, London, W11 1AP, UK
Tel +44 (0)207 313 3918
louiseewington@pngcp.com

Sharing of Ministries Abroad (SOMA)

Revd Stephen Dinsmore, National Director, SOMA UK, PO Box 69, Merriott, TA18 9AP, UK
Tel +44(0) 1460 279737
www.somauk.org
info@somauk.org

South Africa Church Development Trust

51 Heathside, Hinchley Wood, Esher, Surrey, KT10 9TD, UK
Tel: +44 (0)20 8398 9638 / 8699
www.sacdtrust.org

Tearfund

100 Church Road, Teddington, Surrey TW11 8QE, UK
www.tearfund.org.uk

The Scottish Episcopal Church and the Church of Ireland Council for the Church Overseas are also Associate Members of Partnership for World Mission.

Resources for Linking

The following organizations produce excellent resources and are happy to give advice on all aspects of partnership and linking.

BUILD – Building Understanding through International Links and Development – is a network of National and international organizations united around a common purpose; namely to realize the potential of people to bring peace and prosperity through global, community-based partnerships. www.build-online.org.uk

United Kingdom One World Linking Association (UKOWLA) is concerned with sharing good practice in linking with schools, communities, faith, health, local authorities and women. It produces an excellent Toolkit of Good Practice for linking which is available from its website. www.ukowla.org.uk

Further Reading

J. Ayodeji Adewuya, *A Commentary on 1 & 2 Corinthians*, SPCK, 2009.

Daryl Balia and Kirsteen Kim (eds), *Edinburgh 2010 Witnessing to Christ Today*, vol. 2, Regnum Books, 2010.

Stephen B. Bevans and Roger P. Schroeder, *Constants in Context: A Theology for Mission for Today*, Orbis, 2004.

Stephen B. Bevans and Roger P. Schroeder, *Prophetic Dialogue*, Orbis, 2011.

Marianne Bojer, Heiko Roehl, Marianne Knuth and Colleen Magner, *Mapping Dialogue: Essential Tools for Social Change*, Taos Institute, 2008.

Jonathan Bonk, *Missions and Money*, Orbis, 2009, 2nd edn.

Mike Booker and Mark Ireland, *Evangelism – Which Way Now?* Church House Publishing, 2003.

David Bosch, *Transforming Mission*, Orbis, 1991.

Walter Bruggemann, *An Unsettling God*, Fortress Press, 2009.

Stuart Buchanan, *Cross Cultural Christian*, St John's Extension Studies, 2010.

David Cooperrider and Diana Whitney, *Appreciative Inquiry, A Positive Revolution in Change*, Berrett-Koehler, 2005.

Graham Cray, Ian Mobsby and Aaron Kennedy (eds), *Ancient Faith, Future Mission: New Monasticism as Fresh Expressions of Church*, Canterbury Press, 2010.

David Cunningham, *These Three Are One*, Blackwell, 1998.

Andrew Darnton with Martin Kirk, *Finding Frames: New Ways to Engage the UK Public in Global Poverty*, 2010, www.findingframes.org.

Michael Doe, *Saving Power*, SPCK, 2011.

Duane Elmer, *Cross-Cultural Conflict: Building Relationships for Effective Ministry*, IVP, 1993.

Charles E. Farhadian (ed.), *Christian Worship Worldwide*, Eerdmans, 2007.

Damian Feeney, George Lings and Chris Neal, *Mission-shaped Church*, Church House Publishing, 2004.

Paul Fiddes, *Participating in God: A Pastoral Doctrine of the Trinity*, Westminster John Knox Press, 2000.

Walter Freytag, *Mission zwischen gestern und morgen*, Evangelischer Missionsverlag, 1952.

Philip Groves, *Global Partnerships for World Mission*, Grove Pastoral Booklet, 2008.

Christopher Heuertz and Christine D. Pohl, *Friendship at the Margins: Discovering Mutuality in Service and Mission*, IVP, 2010.

Jonathan Ingleby, *Beyond Empire: Postcolonialism and Mission in a Global Context*, Authorhouse, 2010.

Philip Jenkins, *The Next Christendom*, Oxford University Press, 2007.

Eleanor Johnson and John Clark (eds), *Anglicans in Mission: A Transforming Journey*, SPCK, 2000.

O. Kalu, P. Vethanayagamony and E. Kee-Fook Chia (eds), *Mission After Christendom*, Westminster John Knox Press, 2010.

Bruce Kaye, *An Introduction to World Anglicanism*, Cambridge University Press, 2008.

Kirsteen Kim (ed.), *Reconciling Mission*, ISPCK/United College of the Ascension, 2005.

Kirsteen Kim, *Joining in with the Spirit*, Epworth, 2009.

Kirsteen Kim and Andrew Anderson (eds), *Edinburgh 2010: Mission Today and Tomorrow*, Regnum, 2011.

J. Andrew Kirk, *What is Mission? Theological Explorations*, Darton, Longman and Todd, 2002, 2nd edn.

Mary L. Lederleitner, *Cross-Cultural Partnerships: Navigating the Complexities of Money and Mission*, IVP, 2010.

Richard Lewis, *When Cultures Collide: Leading Across Cultures*, Nicholas Brealey International, 2010, 3rd edn.

David Maranz, *African Friends and Money Matters*, SIL International, 2001.

Marcel Mauss, *The Gift*, Norton, 1990.

Henri Nouwen, *Reaching Out: The Three Movements of the Spiritual Life*, Image Books, 1975.

Daniel O'Connor, *Three Centuries of Mission*, Continuum, 2000.

Cyril C. Okorocha (ed.), *The Cutting Edge of Mission: A Report of the Mid-Point Review of the Decade of Evangelism*, Anglican Communion Publications, 1996.

Christine D. Pohl, *Making Room, Recovering Hospitality as a Christian Tradition*, Eerdmans, 1999.

Kara E. Powell and Brad M. Griffin, *Deep Justice Journeys*, Zondervan, 2009.

Presence and Prophecy: A heart for mission in theological education, Mission Theology Advisory Group, Church House Publishing, Churches Together in Britain and Ireland, 2002.

Anne Richards with the Mission Theology Advisory Group, *Unreconciled? Exploring Mission in an imperfect world*, Churches Together in Britain and Ireland, 2011.

Anne Richards, John Clark, Martin Lee, Philip Knights, Janice Price, Paul Rolph and Nigel Rooms, *Foundations for Mission: A study of language, theology and praxis from the UK and Ireland Perspective*, Churches Together in Britain and Ireland, 2010.

Paul Ricoeur, *On Translation*, Routledge, 2006.

Dana L. Robert, *Christian Mission*, Wiley Blackwell, 2009.

Nigel Rooms, *The Faith of the English Integrating Christ and Culture*, SPCK, 2011.

Cathy Ross (ed.), *Life-Widening Mission Global Anglican Perspectives*, Regnum, 2012.

Vinay Samuel and Chris Sugden (eds), *Mission as Transformation: A Theology of the Whole Gospel*, Regnum, 1999.

Lamin Sanneh, *Translating the Message: The Missionary Impact on Culture*, Orbis, 2009.

Glenn Schwartz, *When Charity Destroys Dignity: Overcoming Unhealthy Dependency in the Christian Movement*, Authorhouse, 2007.

Brian Stanley, *The Bible and the Flag*, Apollos, 1990.

Brian Stanley, *The World Missionary Conference Edinburgh 1910*, Eerdmans, 2009.

John V. Taylor, *The Uncancelled Mandate*, Church House Publishing, 1998.

John V. Taylor, *The Go-Between God*, Oxford University Press, 1979.

Andrew F. Walls, 'The Ephesian Moment', in *The Cross-Cultural Process in Christian History*, Orbis Books, 2002, pp. 72–81.

Andrew F. Walls, *The Missionary Movement in Christian History*, Orbis, 1996.

Max Warren, *Partnership*, SCM Press, 1956.

Max Warren, *The Christian Mission*, SCM Press, 1951.

Robert Warren, *Building Missionary Congregations*, Church House Publishing, 1994.

Andrew Wheeler (ed.), *Voices from Africa*, Church House Publishing, 2002.

Ralph Winter and Steven Hawthorne (eds), *Perspectives on the World Christian Movement*, Paternoster Press, 1999, 3rd edn.

Tom Wright, *Paul for Everyone: 2 Corinthians*, SPCK, 2004.

Tom Wright, *Paul for Everyone: The Prison Letters*, SPCK, 2002.

Timothy Yates, *Christian Mission in the Twentieth Century*, Cambridge University Press, 1994.

Church of England Reports

A Growing Partnership: The Church of England and World Mission, Central Board of Finance of the Church of England, 1994.

Bishops in Communion: Collegiality in the Service of Koinonia in the Church, House of Bishops' Occasional Paper, Church House Publishing, 2000.

From Power to Partnership, Britain in the Commonwealth, The Church of England in the Anglican Communion, A Report from the Board for Social Responsibility, Church House Publishing, 1991.

Living God's Covenant, Anglican–Methodist Covenant, Joint Implementation Commission, www. anglicanmethodist.co.uk, w

Living Links: Guidelines for Companion Links, Partnership for World Mission, 2001, www. churchofengland/ourfaith/mission/worldmission/companionlinks.

Living Thankfully Before God: Living fairly before each other, House of Bishops, 2010.

Mission-shaped Church, Church House Publishing, 2004.

On The Way: Towards an Integrated Approach to Christian Initiation, Church House Publishing, 1995.

Partnership for World Mission, Report of the Working Party on Relations between the Church of England, the General Synod and the Missionary Societies, Church Information Office, 1977.

Partners in Mission Presentation, GS Misc 151, January 1982.

Sharing God's Planet: A Christian vision for a sustainable future, Church House Publishing, 2005.

'The Future of Partnership', two addresses given by the Rt Revd Chad Gandiya, Bishop of Harare, at the Partnership for World Mission Conference, 1–2 November 2010, www. pwmconference.co.uk.

The Mission and Ministry of the Whole Church, Biblical: Theological and Contemporary Perspectives, GS Misc 854, The Faith and Order Advisory Group of the Church of England, The Archbishops' Council, 2007.

To a Rebellious House, Report of the PIM process in the Church of England, CIO, 1981.

Anglican Consultative Council Reports and Papers

Communion in Mission & Travelling Together in God's Mission, Report of the Inter-Anglican Standing Commission on Mission and Evangelism 2001–2005, The Anglican Consultative Council, 2006.

Bonds of Affection, The Anglican Consultative Council (ACC 6), 1984.

Continuing Indaba, www.anglicancommunion.org.

Patterns of Inter-Communion Mission Relationships, www.anglicancommunion.org.uk.

Patterns of International Mission Structures in the Anglican Communion, Anglican Communion Office, 1999, www.anglicancommunion.org.uk.

Progress in Partnership, Report of the Mission Agencies' Conference, Anglican Consultative Council, 1987.

Other Organizations and Agencies

A Rocha is a Christian environmental and nature conservation movement, www.arocha.org.

Christian Aid, *Working Together, Bible Studies inspired by the Millennium Development Goals*, 2011.

Paula Clifford, *Theology and International Development*, Christian Aid, 2010.

Council for World Mission, a mission agency in the Reformed tradition, www.cwmission.org.

Edinburgh 2010 World Mission Conference, *Witnessing to Christ Today*, June 2010, www. edinburgh2010.org.

G-Code 2000, Report of the Mid-term of the Decade of Evangelism Conference, Kanuga, Anglican Communion Office, 1996.

Global Connections, *Code of Best Practice for Short-Term Mission 2012*, downloaded from www. globalconnections.co.uk/code.

Philippe B. Kabongo-Mbaya, *Study Text on Fullness of Life for the World Alliance of Reformed Churches*, published for the WARC Accra Convention in 2004, www.warc/accra2004.

The Archbishop of Canterbury, *New Perspectives on Faith and Development*, a speech given to the Tony Blair Foundation, 12 November 2000, www.archbishopofcanterbury.org.

The Lausanne Movement, *The Cape Town Commitment: A Confession of Faith and a Call to Action*, issued by the Third Lausanne Congress on World Evangelization, 16–25 October 2010, www.lausanne.org.uk.

The Micah Network, *The Micah Declaration on Integral Mission*, www.micahnetwork..org.

World Council of Churches, Pontifical Council for Interreligious Dialogue and the World Evangelical Alliance, *Christian Witness in a Multi-Religious World: Recommendations for Conduct*, 2011, www.oikoumene.org.

Journals

Jonathan Bonk, Editorial, *International Bulletin of Missionary Research*, vol. 34, no. 3, July 2010, p. 1.

Dana Robert, 'Cross-Cultural Friendship in the Creation of Twentieth-Century World Christianity', *International Bulletin of Missionary Research*, vol. 35, April 2010.

Cathy Ross, 'A Theology of Partnership', *International Bulletin of Missionary Research*, vol. 34, no. 3, July 2010, p. 145.

Philip Thomas, 'How Can Western Christians Learn from Partners in the World Church?' *International Review of Mission*, vol. 92, 2003, pp. 38292.

CPSIA information can be obtained at www.ICGtesting.com
Printed in the USA
LVOW031424060912

297707LV00004B/1/P